EXPOSING LEADERSHIP

Redefining the Top 20 Leadership Traits

by Ted Martin

Copyright © 2008 Ted Martin

All rights reserved.

ISBN: 1-4392-0062-9

ISBN-13: 9781439200629

Visit www.booksurge.com to order additional copies.

EXPOSING LEADERSHIP

Redefining the Top 20 Leadership Traits

by Ted Martin

*Dedicated to the only people who
occasionally let me lead them:
Jack, Leigh, Ford, Nick.
My wife, Pam, not so much.*

Contents

Introduction... ix
Personality vs. Skill Set.. 1
Herding Cows.. 5
Creating the Right Culture...................................... 23
"The Vision Thing".. 41
Passion Lives Here.. 47
"Trust Me".. 51
The Great Communicator.. 61
Team Builder.. 67
Decision Maker/Risk Taker....................................... 75
Prioritization Skills... 85
Business Intelligence... 91
Commitment and Focus.. 97
Toughness... 103
Don't "Widgetize" the Customer.................................. 111
Creates vs. Facilitates Process................................. 117
Know Your Numbers... 121

Adaptability 125
Innovator/Creator 129
Humbleness/Modesty/Humaneness 133
Career Management 139
Summary 145
About the Author 149

Introduction

MY SECOND GRADER is obsessed with a fellow classmate, call him Frankie. Frankie picks what game will be played at recess, Frankie decides what is cool and what is not, Frankie tells others who can be friends with whom. Right now in his life, Frankie is a natural-born leader. My second grader also thinks Frankie is sometimes mean (you do not need to be perceived as nice to be a strong leader; it helps, but it is not required). There is no guarantee that Frankie will continue as a natural leader at age 40, let alone next year in the third grade, or even next month. But right now, Frankie is a natural-born leader.

In my freshman dorm at Washington & Lee University, we had a natural leader call him Arlen. Arlen not only led the floor, he led the whole dorm, all 4 floors. If he played The Marshall Tucker Band, everyone played The Marshall Tucker Band. He was the natural born leader of the dorm, and it was indisputable. By his sophomore year, he was no longer a leader and had lost his following.

A third example occurred at Kellogg Business School. Kellogg believes in promoting teamwork, and this requires group work in most classes. The groups are not assigned, they form naturally. Once a study group is formed, a natural leader emerges in the group. During my 2 year MBA program, the same people consistently emerged as group leaders. I watched some groups tactfully add a "copier, coffee & doughnut" person so that role would not fall to the other members of the group. How did the leader of a group naturally emerge? For the first meeting, the following criteria usually existed:

- The person was viewed as smart
- The person had a well-balanced personality and was well-liked
- The person initiated a plan in the first meeting

The second meeting focused on work results. The leader of the first meeting could lose the leadership mantle in the second meeting if someone else was more prepared, smarter, and asserted himself/herself as the new leader. The plan from the first meeting needed to be viewed as sound in the second meeting for the leader to remain in his/her seat. But by the end of the second meeting, the leader was confirmed.

Leadership is never guaranteed, it always must be earned. It can be lost as fast as it is gained; it can appear in a flash, and disappear equally as fast. From my calculations, fifty percent of all great corporate leaders were never Frankie or Arlen. That's right, they built their leadership skills incrementally, experience by experience. This book is geared to enhancing your leadership skills through hard work. If you are a Frankie or an Arlen and you kept the leadership train going throughout your whole life, be thankful, because over half of all leaders need to work very hard at it. Half of all leaders are born with natural leadership skills and the other half develop them during their career through lots of trial & error. Everyone has some level of natural born leadership skills that can be further developed through career learning. There are great leaders with very little evidence of leadership early in their life, and there are great leaders who started leading in the second grade. Either path can take you to becoming a successful corporate leader.

Personality vs. Skill Set

THERE ARE COUNTLESS great non-business leaders in society, from Cub Scout den mothers, sport coaches, high school principals, ministers, pastors, rabbi's, all the multiple not-for-profit leaders in society; the list is endless. But the profit motive puts a different spin on leadership. Every decision a leader makes in the business world has a fundamental question behind it: will this action ultimately improve sales and profitability? And that is what makes business leadership different than all other forms of leadership. There are also plenty of individual practitioners in the business world who can be extremely successful without leading anyone. You do not need to lead to be successful. Lawyers, accountants, stock brokers, insurance salesman, investment bankers, doctors, dentists, executive recruiters, craftsmen (and a long list of other professions) can be really good at what they do without leading anyone. If they become the head of an office or a firm, then they become leaders.

This book is written for those in the corporate business world who want to improve their leadership skills. If you manage people, your leadership skills are in play. This book is for anyone who manages people or aspires to manage people in the "for-profit" world, from a small group to a Fortune 100 (F100) corporation.

During my 23 years in the executive search business, I have interviewed thousands of business leaders and have compiled notes on the nuances of leadership. I have recorded why leaders failed and why leaders excelled. I have noted what made a leader successful in one company, but fail at the next one. You are probably familiar with the Peter Principle (you will rise to the level of your incompetence), but what makes some leaders never hit the Peter Principle? This book discusses key leadership traits in a practical sense from real examples. These traits fit an entrepreneurial environment as much as the Fortune 500 world, they are just applied differently based on the size of corporation, the group you are leading, and the industry you are in. This book explains what you need to know about each of these traits to keep advancing in your career. It will help you understand what it takes to get to the next level.

Often a leader has all the technical skills but is foiled by his/her personality. Other times leaders will stake their leadership mode on a personality trait, and the lack of fundamentals will eventually doom them to failure. Great leaders employ a blend of effective personality traits combined with great leadership mechanics to create a rhythm for a company.

This book will help you identify your strengths and weaknesses in your leadership profile. Leadership fundamentals and personality traits are intertwined in a complex balance that is hard to pinpoint during success, but easy to assess during failure.

I am not a believer in trying to differentiate between male and female leadership styles. Every individual has their own unique style, and this book targets all leaders. No one has ever statistically proven that one sex is inherently stronger than the other on a leadership trait by trait basis. Across my 23 years of data collection, I do not see a pattern separating male and female leadership personality traits. Yes, we all know the stereotype that women are better communicators and team builders, but my notes do not point to one sex being consistently stronger than the other on any specific variable. People are complex and I cannot find a pattern that would allow me to stereotype male versus female leadership characteristics.

This book will reference multiple failures and successes of leaders without naming companies or individuals. Some examples will be from well-known F500 corporations, other examples will be from $25MM companies. Everyone has an opinion on the cause of failure for a high profile F500 CEO. Understanding why a leader failed provides advice on how to succeed as a leader. Take interviewing as an analogy. It is easy for a senior executive to comment on what he/she did *not* like about a particular candidate after an interview, but it is often very hard for that same executive to explain why they liked a candidate. Thus it is common to hear a reaction such as "I liked him/her," without the interviewer having the ability to articulate *why* the interviewer liked the candidate. And so it goes with leadership; it is much easier to collect notes on why someone failed, and much harder to get the details on why they succeeded. If sales and profitability are increasing, no one is focused on what specific leadership traits allow the CEO to achieve the increases. But if he/she fails, everyone has an opinion on why they failed.

A cluster of leadership traits can carry you forward as a leader, but a weakness in just one trait can stop your ability to get to the next level. To improve your leadership ability, you first need to strengthen any glaring weaknesses and raise that specific leadership variable to a competent or neutral level. Then you need to identify your strongest leadership traits and ride that cluster to the next level. Most leaders get fired when they have a significantly weak variable in their leadership profile. Any one of the leadership variables in this book can cause you to be fired if it is a real weakness. Your personality needs to match your industry. That means you do not need to be the "warm and fuzzy" type to run an investment bank, but you should have some "warm and fuzzy" to run a hospital. Some industries require very fast decision making (a trading firm), other industries provide lots of time to make decisions (consumer packaged goods). Whether you are a F500 CEO or you are in your very first leadership position, this book will help you understand how to become a stronger leader.

Herding Cows

Once you have a good business plan and you have good people, it is effectively managing those people that makes or breaks a leader. A successful leader inherently attracts good talent. People want to be around him/her and believe that their success lies in working for this leader. A successful leader has an uncanny ability to read people and anticipate how they will react. He/she also is a master at rallying and motivating an organization to move in a common direction. People want to be led, and they want to be part of a team. You must give star performers a cause to believe in or they will leave. "B" players will stick around no matter what, but not "A" players. You also must be good at setting realistic but challenging goals. People need to believe they are on a path going up. Your job is to ensure that each person feels as if you are at the helm steering the ship, assuring their career and financial success. One without the other will not work long term. You must make them all feel like the win/win is in place. Your job is to create this perception and reality for them while leading the business, or you won't retain your best people.

"Herding Cows" is much more analogous to managing people than the expression "Herding Cats." While herding cats is unrealistic, herding cows happens everyday on cattle farms. Herding cats implies no one follows you. The norm with cows and people is that a third will follow as told, a third will go a different direction than where you asked them to go, and a third will resist/balk. Every cow herder knows you must first create an incentive for them to follow, such as a wagon full of hay (a bigger bonus and more options). Next, you create consequences if they don't follow, such as a bb gun shot to the flank (a termination warning). You need to build consensus with the herd, which means getting the lead cow/bull to start walking in the right direction (get buy-in from your senior management team). You must also structure the right pace as you create momentum. Go too fast and you risk losing everyone except the front of the herd. Go too slow and others will start meandering off course due to a lack of focus and energy. Set the pace just right (the rhythm of the company) and you have the fewest stragglers (detractors). You will always have some stragglers, but you want them to be the outliers who are not capable of influencing others. If you let the lead "cow" believe that he/she has decided for herself to head the direction you want the herd to go, you have accomplished the same thing you are striving for in managing people. You must get "buy-in" on the decision process and they must believe they helped select their own direction. The business world calls this empowerment. A rancher calls it a cattle drive.

Leadership is about allowing the best people to make the most important decisions. I call a star performer an "A" player, or an "A", and a solid performer a "B" player, or a "B", etc. Decide how many A's and B's you have at each level in your company. An A is a star, a B is a solid performer, a C should be let go. Your direct reports should be all A's, all people you do not want to lose. If an A resigns, a counter-offer is coming to try to keep him/her. Below that level, decide how many B's are allowed at each level of the pyramid. If you ask a CEO whether they would tolerate a B level performer in their company, they all say "No". But 95% of those who said "no" have B players in their company. Often it is built into the fabric of the organization, and there are 25% B players in most large organizations. If you took them all out at once the organization would grind to a halt. Many jobs require a B player, especially when the job has no visible career path progression. Never let a B get promoted to the VP level, because B's promote B's. Do not let a B person win a political battle over an A. It takes your involvement, and you must be very hands-on to measure people weekly, monthly, quarterly, and annually. Use the "Intensive Care" approach for B's. Intensive care is the opposite of empowerment. It means you don't let a B make a decision without your review when that person is in Intensive Care. This will cause the person to look heavily on the outside to escape the microscope. Terminate B performers inside 6 months if the position they occupy should be filled with an A. Remember that "where there's smoke, there's fire." If you see "smoke", drastically increase the accountability factor on that person. Intensive Care means they cannot breathe without you knowing about it. Many organizations have a pyramid structure designed to weed out the B's at the right level in their career. The brand management pyramid is a great example of a structure that self-selects at every level. Keep in mind that an A performer at the brand manager level can become a B at the group product manager level, and an A at the group manager level can become a B at the director level, etc. The constant measurement of leadership skills is required to assess a person's ability at each level. Top leaders follow the following tenets:

No blind loyalty. View each person as "only as good as their current position." People evolve, they get promoted beyond their capabilities, things happen in their personal lives. Do not assume that once a star, always a star. Sure you have perceptions formed from past performances, that is why you promoted the person. Measure the person in their new position as if you hired him/her from the outside. They will manage more people as they move up, and each level of people management is a new skill set.

Persuade versus dictate. Dictators are "old school" from a style standpoint. But don't forget you are in charge.

If you go too far on the empowerment side, your direct reports will try to fill any perceived leadership vacuum. Make sure you hold people accountable while you empower them. It takes both at the same time to be effective.

Do not worry if people don't like you. You should care a lot if you are respected. Many leaders fail because they try and please too many constituencies, which equates to an inconsistent strategy. If you are promoted from your peers and try to remain friends with the previous peers, you will fail as a leader. No one will respect you if you are influenced by the most recent visit from a former peer. Stick with your vision/strategy, not your previous relationships. Look at results, not how someone makes you feel. The profit motive means you need to rise above personal bias and idiosyncrasies. If you have 3 stars named John, Mary, and Steve and their performance is equal, you will gravitate to the star you personally like the best for promotion first. That is human nature. The flaw is if you have a star you can tolerate, and a B player you really like, and you let the star leave the company and allow the B to be promoted. So the bottom line is that you must stay objective and get rid of your need to be liked. You are not running for office. If you need to be liked, you will fail. You must be respected, and you must win that respect. Respect comes from making tough decisions, the ones that are right for the business. The A players will appreciate your objective decision-making and what they learn from you. Don't try and become personal friends. It is fine if it naturally occurs, but it ultimately will get in the way more than it will help.

Stay emotionally detached. Part of managing people is the ability to pull away from any given person, at any given time, for any given reason. A lot of leaders start to believe the niceties and small compliments that constantly flow their way. Your direct reports understand that compliments and flattery make people feel good. But if you fool yourself into believing them, you will be in for an emotional let down when you are faced with a resignation you never expected. Loyalty only goes so far, and it is about their career, not yours. Stay objective and don't forget that part of their ability to play successfully in the corporate world is making you feel good as their leader. If you take a resignation personally, you allowed yourself to get sucked into the rhetoric and you started believing it was all about you versus them. I interview a lot of leaders who believe their own rhetoric. They forget what it was like when they reported to the CEO, how they actually felt. The rhetoric is critical to building a culture, but only one of your direct reports can become the next president, and everyone is hedging their options. Make sure you have put your arms around the stars and tell them they are in line for the next promotion. It means a lot to a person when they believe they know where they are going. But don't be shocked when you promote one and lose three. If you expect three stars who are ready for a GM role to stick around because you have a great rapport with them, you are naive.

The empowerment reversal. I also see a lot of direct reports who believe all the positive rhetoric coming their way. They start to think they are more important to the organization than any one person could ever be to a company. And when they draw a line in the sand with their boss on a major decision, they are dumbfounded when they are shown the door. They are completely blind-sided. Everyone is replaceable, no matter how great you are told you are.

An example: the head of sales is a star and is put on a pedestal and told he is the "golden one". The company is growing, and the CEO constantly applauds the accomplishments of his sales leader. Subconsciously, the sales leader starts to believe he is the most important person in the company. He starts to believe the company would go nowhere without his sales leadership. He is featured in a newspaper article as one of the city's top performers. This sales leader is now feeling very big. He decides to dig his heels in on a major strategic decision with the founder/owner/CEO, and says "it's my way or the highway." He landed on the highway so fast he was stunned.

Another example: a head of acquisitions for a company believed he was empowered to do deals without running them by the CEO/founder. When he was reined in by the CEO, the head of M&A said "I can't work this way!" So the CEO/founder fired him, resulting in shock and disbelief for the head of M&A.

If you are the CEO in each case, you allowed the individual to truly believe that he/she was bigger than the corporation. In each case, both stars were great employees, but both drew a line in the sand and dared the CEO to step over it. Don't let a star get to the point where they believe they are more important than everyone else. Part of being a great leader is the art of keeping stars humble while telling them how important they are at the same time. You should tell stars they are part of the high potential group, that they will be promoted. If you just tell them how great they are with no context, you are setting them up to draw a line in the sand and lose them.

If you followed the press on the negotiations between Joe Torre and the Yankees post-World Series in October of '07, you could read along and witness the classic difference in paradigms from both sides. Torre came to the table focused on his 12 year track record with the Yankees. Steinbrenner came to the table focused on failing to make the World Series in 2007. Your direct reports will always focus on what they believe they have done for you over their entire tenure, and you as their manager will always focus on what they did for the company this year. You will believe they are only as good as their most recent mistake; they will believe they are as good as their best year ever, in spite of what current year results might show. Your biggest challenge as a manager is to bridge the gap between employee perception and your perceptions. It means Steinbrenner should have (maybe he did, who knows) reinforced all year, every month, that failure to make the World Series would affect the terms of Torre's future contract. That is how explicit you must be, and sometimes it still doesn't work! But don't lose the person over assumptions. You must communicate what is painstakingly obvious to you on a consistent monthly basis to make sure you are heard, and at some point, it also needs to be in writing.

Trust your instincts. You will have an early sense for whether someone is going to make it or not. Use the 6 month rule. Your impression over the first 6 months on someone's capabilities is rarely wrong. If you personally like someone, you can fall into the trap of believing they will grow into the job. Stay objective. As soon as you know in your heart that someone doesn't have what it takes to get to the next level, let them know and begin a transition now, not 6 months later. They are blocking someone who *can* get to the next level. Don't let consensus make a decision. Consensus will evolve to "group think". At the end of the day it is your decision. And don't use the "stall tactic" to let things work out. That is called ducking your responsibility as a leader, and you will never be respected for hands-off policies. Step in and make the call. 95% of the time, if you feel someone will not make it, you will be right. Cut your losses early and save the frustration and stress that will develop as you take too much time confirming your original gut instinct. Trust your gut. People can grow but rarely change.

Hold people accountable. Measure the results accurately and fairly. Make it clear what the expectations are and what the ramifications are if the goals are not met in the stated time frames. If you can't do this, you can't lead. The best leaders use empowerment as a tool to hold people accountable. If you don't hold people accountable, empowerment won't work. Let them develop their own goals first, you need to see how they think. Do not tip your hand on what you think their goals should be. You will learn a lot about them by telling them to go first on the goal setting. Set the accountability rules and the time frame, and document it. Then make it obvious when someone doesn't make their numbers, and establish the consequences upfront. If an A player makes a mistake, use it to coach and develop. If a B makes a mistake, point the finger if you are trying to move the person out of the organization or use the mistake to move them into Intensive Care. Accountability means it is a Zero-Sum game. Zero-Sum means someone is at fault, there is no "things just went wrong." The leader that embraces the Zero-Sum game establishes 100% accountability. He/she believes that things don't just happen; the blame and the reward must be accurately assigned.

Get into the trenches. It's easy to stay above the fray and let them slug it out in the trenches. But in the end, you will be viewed as failing to set behavioral norms for the firm. It may have been a "free for all" when you were down there, but did you respect the boss who let it go on? No, so don't let it go on below you. Wade into the details and make the calls. It is the only way to figure out who is making a mess and who is a victim of the mess. It can feel like baby-sitting at times, but it is the only way to really learn about your people. You must have the stomach and the patience to resolve the "he said-she said" internal battles that happen every day in every company.

Coach and advise. Don't baby sit or dictate. Let them accomplish what they set out to do. Provide direction and advice when it is sought.

Reward excellent performance. Constantly give praise to those who deserve it. Recognition goes a long way in conjunction with financial rewards. The best people must receive the highest pay. If you do not create a meritocracy, your stars will leave. Everyone beneath you in an organization understands the pecking order of talent. If you create a socialistic pay structure (e.g. the old commercial banking paradigm), you are guaranteeing a loss of your A talent, plus lots of apathy and sarcasm.

Avoid hypocrisy. A complete open door management style does not work. You must cut off your accessibility in order to get work done. So don't say one thing and do the other. Don't claim you are "open door" when someone must schedule a meeting to see you. Effective leaders open the door on their own terms and accurately communicate how much the door is open. You can't afford to be interrupted all the time. Truth and consistency are what earn respect. People want their leader to act like a leader and they will watch you like a hawk. They will know what you do. Your body language and eye contact reflect your interest in that person. If you turn away from your computer screen and swivel your chair to directly face the person in your office to make eye contact, you are communicating that this person has your undivided attention. If you do a lesser version of any of these, you are communicating to this person that he/she only warrants half your attention. Use this communicating pattern to make sure people understand your level of openness.

Create managerial incentives that make people want to work for you. Create an attractive workplace. Publicize how happy your people are, create awards and recognition. Tell the employees that it is a great place to work. Always be polite and respectful toward others. Strive to create a unique culture with distinctive attributes, something employees can share with friends, something they can brag about.

Be careful with corporate events. Most corporate events/functions that are designed to build loyalty and camaraderie only work if the following are true:

- The event is held during business hours. If you hold the event on the weekend or at night, (e.g. company picnic) the attendance needs to be optional.
- The event is perceived as fun, entertaining, or provides valuable information.
- The event provides a free give-away, such as food or entertainment value.

If the event costs the employee something to attend (e.g. babysitting cost, extra train fare, parking cost, or the cost of buying a gag gift) the event will be met with resentment. If you make the event optional to attend people will come only if they perceive value for themselves and their families. Most spouses have low interest in attending a corporate event.

Team building events can also be a waste of time and money. Putting a senior management team through a ropes course does not translate into better business performance. People get to know each other naturally over time. Don't force bad events because you think it is what you are supposed to do as a leader. Yes, you should hold functions, but make sure they are well thought out and well received. Almost every employee can cite an event that they considered to be an imposition and a waste of time. Better to schedule nothing than to schedule a bad event. Beware that every function will run its course and lose momentum over time. Everyone eventually burns out on the annual picnic, no matter how good it was the first year.

Assessing your managers. Once you understand each person's capabilities, you can now assess their speed/work ethic. A brilliant strategic thinker who is lazy, works slowly, and goofs around is a B. Likewise, an above average intellect who works hard and is always focused could be an A. If you have a B player (in terms of capability), who does not work hard or fast, you need to move them out ASAP before they affect everyone else's view of the caliber of people you employ. And the only way you know what you have is to immerse yourself in the business and your direct reports. If you want to get fired as a leader, do the following: (1) Have no idea that one of your direct reports is viewed as a suck-up, a slacker, or incompetent by the rest of your team. (2) Let the direct reports fight it out on political issues versus you setting the ground rules, parameters, and behavioral norms. Everyone knows that a problem person beneath you sucks up all your energy. The faster you get rid of the problem, the faster you return to a good nights' sleep. Start laying the groundwork as soon as you wake up at night thinking about a person. The rule of thumb is that a person or issue can wake you up in the middle of the night once, not twice. You must collect data, gather facts and input, and create an action plan the next day. If you need to remove a person, you need to make them realize it. Unless you are going to make sure you have the replacement all lined up before you let the person go, in which case you don't want the person to know you are looking on the outside. If you are afraid of the business ramifications of this person leaving before you are ready with the replacement, and you are going to hunt for their replacement behind their back, you better have thick skin. If/when the person finds out you were searching for a replacement behind his/her back, and your vision/mission statement has the word "integrity" in it, be prepared for some negative feedback.

Don't pick favorites in public. As a good leader and manager, you can never visibly pick favorites. You will always like to work with some people more than others, it is human nature. You must appear to be neutral and biased only by results. At bonus time, base it solely on performance.

Never look like you don't care. Showing indifference to individuals beneath you or to the organization will destroy your culture. A good leader will feign interest even if his/her mind is elsewhere. If you preach passion, you can never come across as indifferent when someone below you is passionate. Your job is to create and facilitate passion.

Never expose compensation differences. Everyone is convinced that everyone knows how much everyone else is earning. If you have a good culture and a close-knit team, people are likely to share compensation data. It does not need to be leaked by accounting or HR; assume the information will leak out once peers become friends. So you better be accurate on rank ordering the team, and you better have the guts to take a stand to reward the stars, at the risk of alienating a B performer who learns that his/her bonus is 25% less than an A-level colleague. People need to believe they have a financial upside based on performance. Once this compensation faith is gone and people believe compensation is not fair, the employees are motivated to look elsewhere for a position.

Don't lose you're "A's". It is much easier to replace a B than it is to replace an A. If you lose an A, you made a mistake. The tough part is that you cannot tell a B that they are a B. The B player does not know or believe that he/she is a B, just like people who procrastinate do not know they procrastinate. The performance review of a B is full of "meets expectations". But the B believes that everyone is getting those marks, not just him/her. The A is receiving "exceeds expectations".

Don't flirt. I have witnessed numerous leaders flirt with the most attractive person in the office. Many do it subconsciously and have no idea that it is obvious to everyone else observing the behavior. It is no longer an accepted part of corporate culture, and can lead to a sexual harassment accusation. You will lose the respect of the organization, and you are no longer viewed as progressive as soon as it is observed.

Don't talk BS. Don't say things like "I hire people smarter than I am." If that is the case, why don't you give them your job? No one believes you mean it anyway, which means people now view you as "full of it". Be very careful to avoid over-promising things to people. You might think it is no big deal, but they will never forget it. You must release the right amount of information at the right time. It takes courage to say "I don't want to answer that right now," versus saying something you will regret later just to keep the meeting moving forward. Under promise, over deliver.

Learn to trust and empower. Paranoia and mistrust often accompany first time GMs, and it never leaves some of them. If you always operate from the wrong side of the fear equation, here is where you will be stuck:

- As a micromanager
- Only able to use a stick, never a carrot
- Never giving someone the benefit of the doubt
- Believing you must constantly push people to get their best work
- Unable to empower

Higher leadership responsibility means more people under your supervision. The more people you manage, the less hands-on you should be as your leadership style adapts to the number of direct reports, layers, and total number of employees. One of the toughest things to learn is how much to increase your empowerment as you move up and manage more people. If you can't let go, you will bottleneck the organization. If you over-empower, decisions will be made below you that you should have made. If one of your best resigns, ask which way you are erring in your management style.

Instill passion. Give your employees something to believe in. Get fired up, and make sure they see you are fired up. If they think you don't care, why should they care? They must believe that you eat, sleep and breathe the business, then they will do the same.

Creating the Right Culture

As a leader, you must match the company's performance measurement system to its culture. If you run a conservative traditional corporation with a "family" culture, chances are there are plenty of mediocre performers who have been embraced by the culture. If you suddenly implement a Bell Curve rating system that requires a manager to fire the bottom 10% of performers, you will create instant chaos. You are now changing a culture, and you better be sure that was your intent. The organization you lead has learned to operate with 20% B performers, and they are now being told they are no longer wanted. They are all friends, the workforce is now rattled and productivity grinds to a halt. Unless a company is going under, leaders must evolve a culture over time to allow natural attrition to occur as part of the process. Co-workers always naturally bond and become friends, and they do not measure each other as an A or a B unless they overlap in their day-to-day work. They create loyalty bonds that are hard to break. When their favorite lunch partner gets fired, they get upset and productivity, loyalty, and motivation all drop. You must do a great job of communicating how things are going to change and why. Explain the cultural evolution is coming before it arrives. You own the culture. If you don't lead it, others will. If you don't establish the ground rules, you are making others fight it out below you. Don't leave a cultural void. The fights could damage an A player, or give life to a B player who should be on the way out.

Be careful in trying to create a cultural image for yourself. Many CEOs fly a corporate jet, yet when they drive a car to work they park in the general lot versus having a reserved parking space upfront. Why? They are not fooling anyone. They are not flying commercial like everyone else in the company, so no one cares if they are parking with everyone else. You will not pick up "community" points on the parking, which is visible every day, if you have a corporate jet. The separate CEO parking space is a bad idea because it provides the rest of the company with a quick way to know if you are on the premises or not on any given day, as well as what time you arrived and departed. If you are the first to arrive and the last to depart, then go ahead and telegraph your parking space. If your hours are variable, a car service circumvents telegraphing your arrival and departure. For the F500, the best solution is general parking for the senior management team, and a car service for the CEO. With a car service no one gets an easy check on whether you are on-site or not. It may seem superficial, but employees will chart your arrival/departure times. Corporate America is not a socialistic experience, and all employees will view any veiled attempts at socialistic behavior with cynicism. Everyone wants to move up, to get to the next level, including a front row of parking. If you give the senior management team a first row of parking, people will aspire to get there. Same with standing in line in the cafeteria. The executive dining room is appropriate in any business with customers who like to be entertained. You need a place where you can host clients/customers. You will not pick up "brownie points" by eating in the cafeteria with the employees. More power to you if you like to do it, but don't do it if you think you are creating an image of being "one of the employees". You will not get the credit if you are doing it for image reasons. Take a look at your company benefits – they are not the same as the level below you. Take a look at the stock/option package you receive versus one level below you. If you want to keep cynicism out of the company, avoid appearances of equality that are not real. If you want to mingle, walk the halls and ask people what they are working on. But you must linger long enough to have a real conversation. I know a F500 leader who likes to walk the halls as a supercharged cheerleader, but the quick one liners become old really fast. His quick "rah-rah" lines have become fuel for sarcasm. He does not stick around to hear a real answer, so he gets superficial responses, such as "we are kicking it today!" And he walks on down the hall as he says "that a way!" You must also create a culture of openness, where there are no back room deals. Get the business chit-chat out in the open, and push down hard on political types who undermine the openness. Root out the double standards that will lead to sarcastic comments behind your back.

Let's take office chairs as an example. In a large company, the purchasing/procurement department is in charge of buying chairs. A person who makes $200,000 a year sits in a chair decided upon by a purchasing manager who makes $50,000 a year. So let's say Purchasing decides on a $150 vs. a $400 chair. They bought the $150 chair X 1,000 people, but the $400 chair is a much better chair. You now have 1,000 unhappy people because you make them sit in a chair that has no image, no "hip", and a lack of features and comfort compared to the $400 chair. Let's say you just presented to the sales force and you told them they are the best sales force in the industry. They are the stars. Then they go back to their desk and sit in a B-grade chair. That does not work. It is an example of overempowerment, where too much decision-making was pushed down with no check on the decision. If you want to kill a culture, cap the hotel and meal expenses for top sales reps, and put your future leaders in cheap chairs. If you cap expenses on your sales/business development people and push them out of Hiltons and into Hampton Inns, you no longer support the rhetoric that they are the best. How could "the best" be staying at a Hampton Inn? And you will lose your top sales people. You tell them they are the best, the superstars, and then they check into their B-grade hotel. It does not work. It's one thing if you explain to them that buying cheap chairs will increase their bonus or the value of their options, but if you make that claim, it needs to be true at the end of the year. You can only cut expenses if employees understand the potential link to a better bonus. If you give the sales rep his/her own P&L, now they can make their own decision on how much they want to spend on lodging.

Many corporate culture traditions are bad ideas that no one has ever challenged. An example is a F100 company where all the senior management team had to do their own PowerPoint presentations. They would spend hours working on their presentations with no outside technical assistance. They all thought it was a waste of time, but it was based on tradition, and no one was brave enough to challenge the status quo. Because the company sold a technology product, the senior management team was supposed to be technically adept with PowerPoint. It made no sense and cost them all lots of time, but it was a tradition the CEO believed in, so everyone complied. As soon as a new CEO was named, he quickly changed the culture and explained that the administrative staff was there to help with presentations.

Another example is the pizza birthday lunch. Every company establishes a pattern of how it deals (or doesn't deal) with birthdays. The decision not to recognize them is the norm in large corporations, but what happens when smaller groups start to create their own celebrations? You must be clear on policies, and you must be consistent. I watched a new CEO decide to order pizza for the senior management team of a $50MM business because it was someone's birthday. Major mistake. He broke the cultural norm (they were never recognized before), and now every member of the senior management team expected a free pizza lunch party in their honor. Where does the "senior management team" status end, meaning how far down do the pizza parties go? He created a small diversion right away that undermined his credibility. He did not think through what he was doing, and he lost credibility as soon as the next birthday of a senior management team member came and went with no pizza party. Bad judgment, bad omen, and he was fired by the Board in his second year. He was not fired over pizza, he was fired for disrupting a culture without improving results. There is no such thing as a free error, all your decisions will be scrutinized by the employees, all the time.

Define your corporate image and personality. Do not promote or tolerate politics, backstabbing or office gossip. The simple rule is to never talk about someone unless it is positive. Set the dress code and values. Support parts of the culture that work and change the dysfunctional parts. Be clear on what behavior you will tolerate or not tolerate (e.g. swearing, sexist comments, racism, etc.). Everyone will mimic your style and follow your lead. Whenever I run into a senior management team that swears a lot, I strive to meet the head of the group or leader, because I can guarantee you that person is swearing a "blue streak". Imitation is the sincerest form of flattery. If you swear, they will swear. You treat people well, they will treat people well.

Create a "No Fear" culture. There are two kinds of fear that are found in every corporate culture. One is the right kind of fear, the other is the wrong kind of fear. The kind of fear you want in your company is the same kind of fear that Andy Grove talks about in his book, "Only the Paranoid Survive." It starts with you at the top, and you need to exude the fear of losing ground to competitors, the fear of not winning the next big sale or contract, the fear of losing a key customer, the fear of not delivering exceptional value, the fear of not driving hard for better performance. Included in this type of fear is the fear of failure, both personal and corporate. Those are the fears you want in your company. You want your direct reports to be afraid of not winning, as compared to being afraid of delivering bad news (wrong kind of fear). You have seen the t-shirts that read "No Fear". Everyone has fear, it is simply a matter of degree as well as a question of whether fear is used as a motivator for excellence, or as a barrier to delivering bad news.

Cynicism and sarcasm. Two of the biggest killers of a corporate culture are cynicism and sarcasm. Once you let them in, the odds of driving them out are slim. If you get promoted or recruited into a business where they already exist, you have 1–2 months maximum to crush them. If you don't make a dramatic example of changing the culture quickly, your window of opportunity will be closed after the first three months. Make an example out of an offender, or you have no chance of ridding the organization of the most damaging elements that undermine everyone's ability to perform for the common good of the company.

Table – pounders dilemma. If you pound the table, yell, berate, etc., you create an environment where that behavior has been established as acceptable. That means your direct reports will carry out the "Kick the Dog" syndrome. The last guy in line goes home and "kicks the dog," because there is no one below him/her to pass on the culture of outward anger. If you chastise, berate, reprimand, criticize, etc., that is how you foster an environment where the cover-up is going to take place. Once the cover-up becomes a normal part of your culture, you are heading toward the worst case scenario, which are false numbers being reported. If you create enough of the wrong kind of fear, you will never hear bad news, and your financial statements will be a mess as the "cover up" seeps into the financials.

Lonely at the top. You cannot be completely open and honest with employees all the time, which is why it is lonely at the top. That is why organizations like the YPO (Young Presidents Organization) exist. Many CEOs don't have time to make friends, and the YPO brings together like-minded CEOs who are very driven and want a social network of peers. They learn from each other, and a key part is getting solace from peers and recognizing there are a lot of people doing the same thing. It also provides a forum to compare "best practice" business issues and personal topics. They learn from each other. Many CEOs put so much into their business that they develop personal issues on the non-work side related to marriage, children, etc. The YPO becomes like a family to them. If you feel lonely at the top, you need to join a network like YPO, TEC, or the Strategic Coach to help you keep perspective.

Friend or boss? Many leaders want informal camaraderie with their direct reports but you can't "have your cake and eat it too." If you drop the barriers too far, they will lose respect. Let's say your direct report plays tennis and he/she is better than you. You are kidding yourself if you believe that a direct report will play tennis against you the same way as he/she will play against a non-boss. Yes, they will let you win if it is close.

Do you work hard? You must be highly visible as the leader in your company. That means physically and mentally visible. The physical part is walking around and being seen consistently on the premises. The mental part is creating a presence in employee's minds. You want them thinking "what would the CEO do?" Not only are you responsible for creating the work ethic standard in the company, you are responsible for creating the operational speed of the company. How fast things get done is a direct reflection of your expectations (assuming you enforce accountability) and how fast a pace you personally set. You must show others the speed at which you accomplish tasks, and how hard you work. You must know when to drop everything for the sake of a corporate issue. Even as the CEO, you need to know when to flex your schedule for an important issue. I know a F500 CEO who always took a lot of trips: golf, fishing, hunting, and skiing. This was accepted practice in the 1980s, but after the 2001 economic slump, times demanded an "all hands on-deck" approach. The inability of this CEO to cancel some trips and show a commitment and recognition to the changing business climate led to his termination by the Board.

Pay your people well. Many companies rationalize why they are going to pass on the best talent in the industry, when the real reason is compensation. One of the biggest, boldest moves you can ever make as CEO is to change the comp structure in your company so you can go after the best talent in the industry. Most leaders are unwilling to rock the boat and will continue to pay lip service to the concept of hiring the best talent. The best talent is almost always the most expensive talent unless you drop down a level of experience. Let's assume Pepsi wants to hire the CFO from Coke. Pepsi must expect to pay more than the current CFO of Coke makes today. So the incentive for the CFO of Coke to leave and to go to Pepsi must include a significant financial upside. This might sound obvious, but you cannot attract an A player with a B compensation package. We see it all the time in the search industry, where a company writes a job description with an internal compensation range that is a lateral move for an outside star. Stars do not move for lateral compensation packages. The best way to load your company with B- grade talent is to have a rigid compensation structure that is at odds with the market for attracting the best talent. Don't focus on the compensation studies, look at what your best competition is paying their best people and what it would take to attract their talent. That is the real life market study that will help you put your compensation in line with "Best in Class". I understand large companies must have compensation programs. But if you do not benchmark from the best company in your industry, you are not in a position to recruit the top talent from that company. What would it take to hire a star from the best company in your industry? If you cannot afford to do it, you are at a long term disadvantage, because they can afford to hire your best people to their company. Many companies claim they want the best when the reality is that their compensation structure requires them to hire either an A talent with much less experience and a steep learning curve, or a B talent with the equivalent amount of experience they are seeking. This dynamic is good for up and coming candidates who interview well and can make a significant career leap on the experience side. In this case, the company and the candidate are sharing the risk. The company is hiring someone who must grow into the position and who has not done it before. The candidate is taking the Peter Principle risk. The candidate may have just jumped their career too far above their ability level and not be afforded the time by the hiring company to perform at an A level.

Political skill is one of the most underrated and least discussed aspects of leadership. You must be able to identify political animals, power brokers, neutrals, and back-channels in the organization. Sometimes getting "buy-in" from all the key parties is the most critical aspect of moving an idea forward. Whether you are the CEO or the sales leader with a new commission structure idea, you must present the idea at the right time, on the right platform, in the right way. Your job is to give your boss credit while you are below, and then push the credit down once you are above.

One of the key actions you must take as a leader is to get rid of any customs and traditions that impede the efficiency of getting things done. If you came up through the organization, this is your chance to change the processes that waste people's time. Move at the right pace to create the change. Make sure everyone understands why a certain report is no longer being produced. Give people a chance to convince you the report is of value. Try to get rid of every established meeting. Do not worry about high resistance, only reinstate the meeting if there is no better way to move the business forward. This is your chance to decrease politics and bureaucracy, and the only way to do it is to create ways for people to speak openly about a business issue without being sacrificed. If there is a culture of mutual protection, it is very hard to break it. You must recalibrate the whole company around the notion of increased bonuses and stock value tied to performance and openness. You must convince them that openness leads to better efficiencies, which leads to better profits, which leads to higher compensation per individual. The toughest part is to create these links in the organization if they do not already exist. And it is really tough to get it down to the "factory floor" or administrative level.

Perception becomes reality. Several years ago, I was waiting in the airport to board a delayed flight. The pilots of this airline were publicly disgruntled, the flight attendants were threatening a strike, and all the acrimony was in the press everyday. So I walked up to a group of three pilots and we started talking. The pilots were convinced they were "being ripped off" by senior management. When I questioned the value of their options over the past 12 months they had no idea if their options had increased in value or not. Clearly the CEO had been unsuccessful communicating to the pilots. The pilots' options had actually increased in value, but the pilots had no idea, and they were convinced they were being taken advantage of by senior management. Over the next few weeks I started asking flight attendants of the same airline (on different flights) what they thought of their CEO. They each independently related the same story about how the CEO had once flown on a trip and had treated the flight attendants very poorly on the flight. The story was circulating like wild fire among the flight attendants. But not one flight attendant who reiterated the story ever knew a flight attendant who was actually on the specific flight with the CEO when the rudeness occurred. It was a rumor gone wild, but perception becomes reality. So when it came time for union negotiations, this CEO already had the flight attendants against him. And the pilots decided they were being treated unfairly because of the belief that the CEO did not care about their partners, the flight attendants. I then called a member of the senior management team and he acknowledged they knew about the rumor but they could not stop the rumor. A classic case of the lack of communication with misinformation filling the void. How many times have you heard of factory workers voting to not give any concessions, even though it means they will be out of jobs? You've got to find a way to creatively break through with communication to change the views that are not true. This is your number one goal for breaking the political cultural norms that will hurt the company's profitability.

Every organization has politics within a culture. The better and faster you recognize and identify the unwritten cultural rules of the company, the better you can lead. Failure to lead within the cultural norms of the company can result in a plateaued career at that company. I have listened countless times in interviews to a fired leader bemoaning the fact that the company is moving forward with all his/her ideas, but he/she is no longer with the company. This is very common, where the individual had all the right ideas but lacked the ability to successfully navigate the political waters. And rest assured no one still residing in that company today is saying "too bad about John/Jane, these were his/her ideas." The new leader has adopted John/Jane's ideas as his own and is running with them because he is successfully navigating the political channels. You must identify the accepted way to get things done, even if you are at the top. If you are a CEO, you still report to a Board of Directors, and you still need to be politically correct with the Board.

I know another F100 CEO who always took lots of vacation. The company's performance started to slip, but the vacations kept right on coming as if nothing had changed with the company's stock price. The Board made it clear that these were tougher times that required battening down the hatches, with more hands-on-deck time. But the CEO kept sailing around the world, resulting in his termination. If you don't have good self-perception, you will never pick up on the views of the organization. Political awareness on the outside starts with self awareness. You will ultimately fail as a leader without high self awareness. This particular CEO failed to tack in the changing winds and it cost him his job. He was blind-sided by the termination and was unable to hear the Board telling him that the decrease in company performance was on his head.

You must have a high political antenna. Does this mean everyone should be a political animal? No, it means you are going to be blind-sided if you ignore the corporate politics. There is a famous saying: "With elements of principle, stand like a rock. With elements of style, go with the flow." We are talking here about the "style" of a company, the flow, the way decisions get made and communication is handled. You must understand how to "go with the flow" to communicate your ideas. If you are the leader, you have the opportunity to create your own culture and change the flow. But do it too fast and you will lose everyone. Everyone is accustomed to a certain cultural flow, you must give them time to adapt to your changes.

Let's take dress code. Every company has a dress code, no matter how formal or informal. The subtleties are important to observe. In one F100 company, "mahogany row" wears long sleeved button-down shirts during the summer. The rest of the company wears short-sleeved shirts in the summer. Once you are the CEO, you can pick long or short sleeves and watch your direct reports all mimic your style. If you are the CEO and you alternate between long and short, now you have said either style is acceptable. But if you only wear long-sleeved shirts, I guarantee you that all direct reports will only wear long-sleeved shirts. And if the senior management team is isolated, the "badge" of mahogany row says that you do not wear long-sleeved shirts in the summer until you are promoted to mahogany row. Now most everyone wants to wear short-sleeved shirts in the summer, but in this company that is reversed. Imitation is the sincerest form of flattery, and everyone's political antenna will cause them to mimic your style. Sometimes all the watches are the same style in a senior management team because everyone wears a watch like the CEO's watch. No one wants to stick out, conformity of style is common in the corporate world. Shoes all start to look alike as well. By dressing the same as the leader, you are saying "I am on your team and I proudly wear the team uniform." Even in a start-up company, the same conformity of style exists. It just happens to be very casual versus formal. Wearing flip-flops and shorts in Silicon Valley can be just as much of a corporate uniform and a style conformity as wearing a suit.

Your job as leader is to create a culture where information is shared. Sounds simple, but you are running against the "flattery syndrome". The flattery syndrome means that the organization will have a tendency to feed your ideas back to you, with endorsement and slight refinement.

The Vision Thing

If there was a business game show and they asked contestants, "What is the most important aspect of leadership?" Many would hit the buzzer and yell "Vision!" Is Vision an overrated buzz word or the #1 leadership skill? The answer is that it is both. I see a lot of companies where they trot the "Vision" word out once a year for the annual strategic planning process, but it mysteriously disappears as soon as the first quarter numbers are missed. Without an articulated Vision, people in an organization make an assumption about where the company is going. And if you have eight direct reports, you will have at least three different versions of the company's Vision unless you are the constant and consistent communicator of the Vision. You must constantly communicate the Vision to others, no matter how obvious it is to you. People will forget, and other ideas will mysteriously fill any void. Don't let a void happen, I assure you it will be filled with a different Vision than the one you are failing to communicate. So you should start by creating a Vision and then you rally the organization around that Vision. The problem is that few leaders take it seriously. A Vision that becomes reality is rare. A leader who creates the Vision, implements the strategy and guides the execution is hard to find. Most treat a Vision like a mission statement, meaning they create the plaque or the sign on the wall and then it becomes part of office decoration, guaranteed to show up at any big meeting, like flowers at a wedding. The real challenge is to bake the Vision into the day-to-day running of the business.

If you create a Vision that is off-target, you will be finished as a leader in that company. You must make people below you feel that the best person to think about the business is you. It means you have a level of conceptual thinking ability that impresses people. And you should get the best ideas from the smartest people in the company to shape your thinking. And then you package it just right and "sell it" and everyone believes in you as a leader. Make no mistake about it, your conceptual understanding of the business must be perceived as better than everyone else's. It does not really need to be, but your ability to gather input from the smartest people in the company, pick the right information, and translate it into a Vision statement must be strong. You should absolutely take the best ideas from everyone beneath you and synthesize their views into the Vision for the company. If you cannot own the Vision, you will fail as a leader.

An example: a F500 telecom corporation Board hires a new CEO from outside the industry. The Board is convinced that it is all about leadership skills, that the industry background doesn't matter, so they hired a well-known CEO from a non-tech industry. The problem is that he could not learn the complexities of the fast-moving telecom business fast enough. The bottom line is that he wasn't smart enough to pick it all up in time. He was plenty smart in his old industry that he grew up in, but he ran out of learning curve time in the new company. You cannot create a Vision if you cannot grasp the detail of your company and how it competes across product lines in your industry. This CEO had no shot of creating a Vision for the company (which it badly needed) because he could not understand the business fast enough. I was in the office of a divisional GM at this company when we both saw the new CEO walk by in the hallway. After he had passed, I asked how he was doing. "Dead man walking" was the response from the division president. Why? "He can't follow the strategic issues we are putting in front of him in the Operating Review. His questions have revealed to all the GMs that he is still not up to speed and he has been here three months. The company is frozen until he comes up to speed or is replaced, and all the bets are that he can't come up to speed soon enough. Game over." The CEO was terminated six months later by the Board, as the company continued to wait for him to come up to speed.

Another example: the CEO of a F500 software firm decided to focus his company on a very specific technology application as opposed to being a broad-based solution provider. All his senior management team put their resume on the street as the result of his new Vision, which they all considered to be strategically wrong. He lost his best people and the company revenue growth stalled. The CEO will be gone in 12 months unless he can get a new team to embrace the strategy and prove his Vision is the correct one.

How do you create the right Vision? Good leaders listen to everyone who understands the business they are in: employees, customers, suppliers, distributors, board members, competitors, bankers, lawyers, accountants, analysts, business school professors, private equity investors, etc. Your direct reports are the most important since they better be your smartest people as the result of the pyramid effect. From constant input, you form a plan to improve sales and profitability. Then you package it and sell it internally (and externally if you are public), and never stop selling it as long as it makes sense. A Vision statement does not explain that the company is going to cut costs versus invest in new product development. That is a short-term strategy for the year. Many companies lose their way because the leader does not have a Vision, or the leader fails to believe, communicate, and reinforce the Vision. If you want to find a F500 company in trouble, look for one that claims their Vision statement is to shift from cost-cutting to new product investment spending. When you see reactive knee-jerk shifts in strategy, short the stock. On the other hand, the competitive landscape changes frequently, no matter what business you are in. It is normal to frequently adjust vision/strategy/execution. Business leadership is about taking calculated risks, and the one who makes the best bets comes out ahead. So the bottom line is that your Vision needs to be good, and it needs to be on target to allow the business to grow. And you need to adapt it as soon as the landscape changes. The key to getting the Vision right is being inquisitive. Inquisitive leaders want to know what everyone thinks about their business at all times. They constantly seek input and perceptions from others. You must want to know what others think, and borrow the best thinking. If your thinking is the best thinking, more power to you.

Second grader Frankie (first chapter) does not need to ask the opinion of the other kids, he picks the recess game and everyone else follows. That style of leadership does not work well in corporate America today. Today that is called being a non-inclusive leader with no empowerment skills, and you will lose your best people over time if you are ever wrong. Strong leaders take the best input from everyone else, sense the right direction, and then sell it to everyone else so you are the leader. Otherwise you are not the leader, and you are not going to get to the next level. The "Vision" thing is real, people need one, and don't forget they need to hear it two times more than *you* think they need to hear it. "What do *you* think?" is the best question a leader can ask of his management team, as long as the answers are followed by your ability to clarify and summarize all the best input back to them as the answer.

Passion Lives Here

YOU KNOW WHEN a leader is truly passionate about his/her business. Take Microsoft's Steve Ballmer and his famous "monkey dance" at the annual Microsoft shareholders meeting several years ago. The passion he exuded for his organization was evident, and a video email of his episode made it around the country. While the email made fun of Ballmer, it also generated a tremendous amount of respect among the Microsoft employees because he exuded the passion he wants every employee to have in the company. In 2004, the Democratic Presidential contender Howard Dean released a lot of misdirected passion that was caught on a live microphone, and it cost him the Democratic nomination. Too much passion comes across as obsessed, unbalanced, and slightly crazy. Not enough passion comes across as uncaring, apathetic, hands-off and weak. You must find the balance and walk the razor blade edge.

Leaders must find ways to exhibit passion about their business. Whatever it takes to demonstrate it and influence the organization to share in the passion is essential for success. As a leader, others will reflect your level of passion. But you must publicly show it, and show it in every meeting. With passion comes motivation and intensity. If you are not passionate about the business, get out of the business because the lack of passion will trickle down throughout the organization. If you are not passionate, get out before you fail or you are pushed out.

Many leaders have been known to be so passionate about their business that they identify too closely with their company. They begin to treat the company as an extension of themselves and view using corporate funds for personal use as deserved. Passion without perspective/balance will lead to rationalization and rationalization is the most dangerous partner you can ever have. Most fraud starts with rationalization. And most rationalizations start with over-zealous passion.

Demonstrating passion does not mean you need to jump around the office high-fiving everyone. But it must be very clear to all employees that you are passionate about winning the game of business that you are in. You do not need to have an effervescent personality to exude passion for your business, but it helps. Many leaders are droll at best, but the passion is quite evident. If you tell people you want to win and constantly remind them that you want to win, the passion will be evident. I know many CEOs who do not have much personality, but no one disputes their passion for the business. You don't need to be charismatic to show passion. Charisma makes it easy, but passion comes in the way you approach the business. You get lots of opportunity on a daily basis to display passion to your peers and subordinates and bosses. Take advantage of each chance to send a message. If you don't live, eat, and sleep the business, you cannot convey passion for the business. You can still have life balance and convey that your heart and soul are poured into the company. You can have life balance and still have all your direct reports feel that you "eat, sleep, and breathe" the company. Don't ever try and fake passion, you will lose. It must be genuine. Passion connects you to the business. It is what allows you to be there when a direct report, peer, or boss has a tough business issue. It allows you to be the sounding board or the mentor. It shows you care, it connects you to the rhythm and pace of the business, and it lets people know you want to win. No one wants to be on a team where you can't tell if the leader wants to win or not. If you don't or can't show passion, you cannot create an image. Look at the passion-image of the following companies, where it holds true that if you think of the company, you think of the CEO:

Amazon – Jeff Bezos
Apple – Steve Jobs
Cisco – John Chambers
Dell – Michael Dell

Facebook – Mark Zuckerberg

GE – Jack Welch, now Jeff Immelt

Google – Eric Schmidt

Microsoft – Bill Gates / Steve Ballmer

Oracle – Larry Ellison

Starbucks – Howard Shultz

Trump – Donald Trump

Xerox – Anne Mulcahy

Why don't many of us know the CEO (off the top of our head) of Proctor & Gamble, for example? The company is well known, but not the CEO. The answer is that either the CEO doesn't have the ability to convey passion on the outside, or he chooses not to do so. If you are publicly traded, you have an obligation to shareholders to create outside/external passion to the best of your ability.

There is also a traditional Midwestern value orientation that can keep CEOs from blowing their own horn on the outside. That is one reason why F100 companies like Abbott, Baxter, Eli Lilly, Kraft, McDonalds, Motorola and P&G have lower profile CEOs. The other reason is that technology companies evolve faster and have headline breaking new product news, compared to a new drink flavor. The West Coast clearly has a less traditional means of disseminating information, which also helps the CEOs develop high profiles quickly.

"Trust Me"

Have you ever heard a person tell you they "are about to tell you the truth?" The implication is that they were lying at other times or shouldn't be trusted if they don't say "trust me". If someone tells you how honest they are, they usually have an integrity issue. As a leader, you should never feel compelled to use the words "trust me". You must rely on your actions to build and convey trust. It must be earned over time.

Many strong leaders run companies on a flexible value system. That does not mean dishonesty, it does not mean fraud. It means there are occasional demands to put a certain spin on a business situation. You must often leave out some information. Whether it is conveying new product news for the analysts, telling a subordinate why they will not get the next promotion without having them leave the company, or motivating a sales force, you must be able to decide when you do not disclose everything you know, without it becoming an integrity issue.

On a scale of 1–10, most high integrity business leaders operate in the 7–9 range. I have met only two "10's" in my years and both struggled with working in a corporation due to their inability to be "grey" versus "black and white" when it was needed. Business often requires working in the grey zone. A well-known retired CEO recently said "what we called "managing earnings" in the 1980's is now called fraud." That statement sums up the moving ethical bar in corporate life.

Let's take the practice of "pull-up." In the 1980s, the consumer packaged goods industry engaged in a common practice of shipping product at year-end to their own warehouses (and recording it as revenue sold to customers) to make the year-end numbers. Because everyone did it, no one viewed it as unethical. The product was eventually shipped to the customer in the first quarter of the new year when the customer ordered it, not in December when the revenue was recorded. It was openly discussed in the halls as part of year-end business, and was not viewed as unethical. Today, that is viewed as fraud. Did any CEO of a consumer packaged goods company in the 1980's think they were breaking the law? The answer is no, they were doing what they perceived everyone else in the industry was doing.

Likewise in the pharmaceutical industry, the practice of giving away a free sample to doctors eventually lead to giving away a box of free samples, which allowed doctors to sell free product 100% profit, which equates to bribing doctors.

This was also widespread in the 1980s, and today the CEO could go to jail. No one considered the CEOs of the pharma or consumer packaged goods industry to be unethical because it was the industry norm. Today you would be viewed as a criminal for the same behavior. The landscape changes, and you must change with it. It is extremely hard for most leaders to draw an ethical line that puts their company at a disadvantage to the competition, especially if it is a publicly traded company. It's a different standard than comparing the ethics of non-business people. Take the recent scandal of backdating options. Not only was this commonly viewed as an accepted norm, it was often used as a retention tool for stars. If a top member of the senior management team resigned and you wanted to keep the person, a counter-offer might well have contained price adjustments on his/her options to put value back into their long term option package. Today that is called fraud.

Let's take large service firms in the late 1980s. Large service firms had national contracts with airlines, where they received 20% off the retail price of each flight at the end of the year, as long as a certain minimum level of total flights was achieved by the firm. So the consulting/accounting/search firm thus would make a 20% profit from the reimbursable flights billed to each client as a result of the discount applied at the end of the year. The discount was not transparent to the clients, who unknowingly reimbursed the service firm for more than the eventual actual cost of the flight. To illustrate, a consultant at firm X flies San Francisco – Chicago roundtrip on behalf of Client A. Consultant submits a receipt for a $600 roundtrip airfare, which is reimbursed by Client A for $600. At the end of the year, consulting firm X receives a 20% discount off all flights, thus firm X makes a profit of $120 on that flight. Client A does not know about the reimbursement. Now did this large service firm claim the highest level of integrity? Absolutely. Were there multiple service industries that did the same thing? Yes. So the temptation for the almighty dollar skews the definition of ethics. There are very few "boy scouts" in business because the pursuit of the almighty dollar is too great. I have no idea if any large service firms are still doing it today, but their risk is very high today if they get caught.

Many powerful figures have crossed the line in the last few years. Leaders can remain popular despite marital infidelity. Many leaders have ended their careers and/or are behind bars today because of financial fraud. Martha Stewart was the victim of an age-old stock broker practice of tipping on an inside trade to garner more business from a client. Fifteen years ago she could have bragged about her financial gain at a cocktail party. Today she recently served a jail sentence. The ethical landscape evolves, and you must evolve with it.

Most leaders embrace honesty and integrity at the highest possible level for their industry, both personally and professionally. It is very hard to lead an ethical improvement to industry norms versus follow them. If you follow, you look as bad as the next guy when the rules change. A great way to quickly lose respect in your company is to make exceptions "this quarter" on the ethics that you espoused last quarter. You must consistently define the levels of business ethics for your company and industry. Be consistent with your company code of honesty/integrity. Define where you draw the line and don't make exceptions. Each industry has a different level of ethics. If everyone is bribing for business in a third world country, it can be a hard decision to not do business in that country.

Take the recent Siemens scandal. The bribe system had become baked into the Siemens corporate culture, so that no one viewed it as unethical anymore. Once you rationalize a certain behavior, you cannot get rid of it easily. Everyone on the outside was shocked at Siemens' behavior; everyone on the inside was shocked that their behavior was viewed as highly unethical versus "that's the way business is done". The bribe had become an accepted part of Siemens' culture to get business.

It's very tempting to create the financial picture that investors want to see. Some leaders get to the point where they believe they are above the common value system. They don't believe they need to adhere to corporate policy themselves and they create a double standard. Avoid a star performer who will cut integrity corners, it will catch up to him/her and get you fired when it does. You must look objectively at the value system of your company and industry and decide if it needs an upgrade. The hardest thing is to objectively evaluate long-standing industry customs such as "pull-up", free samples, bribes, or lead paint. The leaders of tomorrow will take an ethical stance <u>above</u> current customs and lead the change for the industry, versus wait for the industry to be policed by an Elliott Spitzer type (how ironic was his fall from the bully pulpit?). Each industry will eventually be examined.

The microscope was recently on the student loan industry and the "bribing" of colleges to guarantee loan volume. The toy companies are under fire for allowing lead paint on their toys. Leaders forget that "the buck stops here". It does not matter if your industry has been covering toys with lead paint for a long time. As soon as your industry is forced to change, you are guilty. Either guilty of an ethics violation or guilty of running a company without knowing what was going on beneath you. You lose either way. Investment banks are full of long standing traditions of internally making money that will eventually not stand up in the post Sarbanes-Oxley world. Plenty of newly defined "fraud" remains in the system. So if you are the CEO of an investment bank, it makes sense to try and lead the industry now versus be punished with everyone else later. If you are privately held, you won't change until you are forced to change. If you are publicly held, you have a double-edged sword at your earnings throat. Change before everyone else and take a quarterly earnings hit, but if you lead the change you will get public kudos and x amount of "goodwill". The profit incentive will be too great to change until the whole industry is forced to change. So you will wait for a level playing field.

A leader who has the gift of generating trust and being trusted will be respected by the organization. If people trust you, they will develop to the best of their ability. Generating trust is not the same thing as 100% honesty. Leaders generate trust by keeping confidence and not reneging on what they promised. Create a predictable style and come through on your promises. Don't change the rules without having a really good macro reason why you are changing the rules. For example, if you change a compensation system (decrease it), you risk losing your top producers. Don't change it unless your costs are too high and you will go out of business unless you change it. Warren Buffet thought he could change the Salomon Brothers' compensation system and he was wrong.

Take the staff meeting as an example. In an environment of "no trust", the leader does all the talking. Everyone else only speaks when they are called on, or when a point is directed to them. All conversation originates and stops with the leader. In an environment of trust, conversations originate and end around multiple functional leaders at the table. When trust is not there, lots of energy is wasted on politics. If people trust you, they will allow you to be human and make mistakes. Not big mistakes, because you are getting the big bucks to make the right calls, take the right level of risk, and improve performance (which means everyone makes more money).

If you are not trusted, ulterior motives will always be assigned to your behavior. Trust is the most fragile of all the variables. Once you lose it, you cannot get it back, it is gone forever until you switch companies. And it is very easy to lose. All you need to do is under-communicate, and have a direct report say "he/she said this, but now we are doing that." Try telling the sales force you have a new bonus structure, and then never implement it. Try telling the employees you are working on higher base salary grades, and then change your mind. Try promising a long term compensation plan, and then take two years to implement it and when you finally do, have it be perceived as a "paper tiger" where no one can really make any more money. Simply say one thing on one day, and say a different version on another day without properly explaining yourself, and you will lose everyone's trust. Promise something to a person, then forget you promised, and you have permanently lost that person's trust. If you make a decision to withhold information, and then that information leaks out another way, you have lost their trust. If you lose their trust, performance must be exceptional to survive as a leader. Most leaders lose trust through poor communication skills versus through an actual direct violation of trust. A very simple way to lose trust is to talk about someone else behind their back. Even if it is positive, it can cause resentment. And if it is negative, all listeners will perceive that you do the same thing to them. Trust is as fragile as an egg, guard it with your career at stake. Stay consistent and do not over promise. Avoid using the words "never" and "always". You are the standard bearer of trust for the company, don't forget it.

Many business leaders give a lot back to society. In spite of the recent government intervention, our free market capitalism structure is still the model for the rest of the world. This chapter points out some of the pitfalls of leadership, but in no way is meant to be condemning of American business.

The Great Communicator

ANY TIME YOU meet with anyone in the organization, ask the person what they are working on, then ask them how it fits the company strategy. There is no such thing as over-communicating the vision/strategy/execution triangle. If you fail to frequently communicate the three legs of this triangle, you will create the business version of the Bermuda Triangle – people will get lost. The difference is that they won't know they are lost, because someone else will have put their own spin on where the business is heading. At a minimum, all employees need to be reminded once a month. Any time the opportunity presents itself to you, address how their work fits the vision/strategy. It's O.K. for vision/strategy/execution to frequently change as long as there are sound business reasons for the change. You must communicate any change with clear explanations for the change.

Start with communicating effectively to your direct reports. The ability to structure a meeting that is not a waste of time, involves everyone, and moves everyone forward is one of the fundamental keys to success. A major flaw is to go through the process of having a staff meeting, but in reality you are running the company in the hallways or via email. This disconnect will cause politics to brew beneath the meeting. Good leaders achieve an openness that allows them to have a meeting that gets everyone on the same page and pushes the tough issues onto the table for discussion. It is easy for the leader to fall into the habit of running a "window dressing" meeting when everyone knows that the tough decisions get made one-on-one with the leader through multiple, informal conversations. Ask people if a meeting was valuable or not, and get rid of all useless meetings. Bad meetings are morale killers for companies. True communication means there are no superfluous meetings where you cannot openly address the tough issues. Talk openly about the business, and people will respond openly to you. The ability to manage up is as crucial as the ability to manage down. Whether you are a CEO communicating to a Board or you report to a boss, you must understand the importance of communicating to your superiors. Everyone has a superior unless you run a private company with no Board and you have no debt. Many CEOs have been ousted by Boards for failing to communicate up.

The real test is whether any of your direct reports can respectfully disagree with you in an open meeting. If you can accomplish an open communication style, you now have the ability to stop breathing your own fumes. Intimidation is the number one cause of stopping open communication that flows both ways. Once you have an environment where no one challenges a false statement by the leader, you have a company that will eventually get into trouble.

Constant feedback is the key to great communication. The ability to give positive and negative feedback on a consistent basis is part of being a great communicator. Communication is not only about being consistent, it is about understanding the ramifications of what you say. Too often leaders fail to comprehend the "ripple effect", meaning the implication 3–4 levels down in the organization of what you just said. You also must communicate the right amount of information. Too much superfluous communication is no different than the age-old adage of "crying wolf". Eventually you will cause people to speed-read your emails or skip your voicemails to listen to them later. Too little communication will cause people to view you as detached from the business or not interested in the details. Every company has a communication flow and it is important for you to establish a consistent pattern. The ability to pick the right communication mix (across email, voicemail, meetings and hallway) and deliver the right amount of communication with the right tone is a critical skill to continue growing as a leader. The communication medium, amount of information, and tone must all be balanced. You must develop a consistent pattern and style of communication so the rest of the organization knows what to expect and how to respond. You must also be able to respond carefully and quickly in an unplanned situation. It starts with being a great listener. A key aspect of being a great listener is accessibility. You must define how accessible you will be as you set the communication standards for the company.

For example, one F500 CEO was notorious for letting everyone know via email that he was a workaholic with no normal life pattern. If you send an email at 2 a.m., you are establishing this as a merit badge of working hard. This will encourage direct reports to act out a similar pattern, such as sending emails at 3 a.m. Make sure you stay consistent on how often you check your email and what merits a response. You must quickly set standards, parameters, and guidelines for how much information is being communicated and how often. Everyone will follow your lead. If someone is constantly sending you too much information and you do not correct them, you are a weak leader and you will be flooded with emails. If the sender is unable to "get the message", put the person under close watch (Intensive Care); they will have trouble following directions in general. Everyone is naturally averse to delivering and receiving bad news. If you foster a closed communications style, significant decisions will be delayed, hurting the business.

Leaders tend to develop a myopic view that the world evolves around them. They learn to communicate one way (outbound) and no longer can pick up feedback like they once could. If you achieve rock star status (like Jack Welch did at GE) it is easy to get lost in the limelight. Here is a quote from a F500 CEO who was forced to resign by his Board: "all my ideas were turning the company around, but the Board said I was out of time. The new guy is simply letting my plan work, and it is working really well. I did a poor job of keeping the Board informed and it cost me my job." If you create a communication void in the company, rest assured that void will be filled by others, and they may not have your best interest in mind. A famous line in business is "the silence is deafening." All businesses rely on knowing what the leader thinks on a constant basis. Many leaders underestimate how closely they are being listened to by all constituents. As a leader, you must figure out how to communicate to everyone, and you need to develop a pattern. A pattern provides comfort and keeps you from being overwhelmed. This pattern is what keeps direct reports from walking into your office every hour, the Board members calling you every week, or the private equity firm asking you for too many conference calls. It is up to you to set the ground rules, and then you must consistently adhere to them. If you break your own pattern, get ready to be flooded by communication coming back at you, as different groups perceive there are new (or no) guidelines. With no guidelines, they will err on the side of over-communicating. By establishing a rhythm and pattern of communication for your company, you allow others to learn the communication rhythm of the company and prove they can fit in. If you are constantly changing the rhythm for no reason, you create lots of room for people to coast. And you create uncertainty around how much they should communicate.

One of the most important points about communication is to make sure your best people know how good they are. Constantly remind your high potentials or your "stars" that they are incredibly important to the future. Tell them they are on the high potential list, that they are going places, and that the financial rewards will be significant for them. You must constantly reinforce a golden path for them, a path of career and monetary advancement. Don't pretend like money isn't important to people, it is extremely important to everyone who works in a for-profit environment. When someone says "its not about the money," that means the money is a very important variable in their decision process. Strong communication means stating the obvious. If you are having a senior management team dinner, you must let them all know that attendance is mandatory. Never assume people heard your subtle hint; you need to constantly communicate a "blinding glimpse of the obvious" on any issue of importance.

Team Builder

I WAS INTERVIEWING A VP of sales on a Monday morning, and I asked him how his weekend went. He replied, "My weekend was ruined. My boss received a call Friday afternoon from an unhappy customer, so my boss left me a blistering voice mail Friday night. Why didn't he wait until Monday? It's not like we can do anything about it over the weekend."

If the VP of sales is very good and the boss wants to keep him, that boss just made a bad communication decision, known as the "Kick the Dog" syndrome. On the other hand, if the boss wants to start positioning the VP of sales for termination, his voice mail timing was appropriate. If he wants to keep him, it was a bad decision on the tone and timing of his voicemail. There are three possible scenarios that reflect this boss's action:

Scenario 1.) The boss didn't think, he just reacted and lashed out at the person ultimately responsible for the upset customer, the VP of sales.

Scenario 2.) The boss is encouraging the VP of sales to start looking outside the organization, he wants him to leave, or doesn't care if he resigns. He has already started a termination file on the head of sales and he would rather have the person leave on his own volition then go through the termination process.

Scenario 3.) The boss thinks highly of the VP of sales, but is truly shocked and enraged that this incident occurred. It is a legitimate screw-up, and his reaction is justified due to the magnitude of the mistake. But the timing should have been held for Monday, unless there really was something the VP of sales actually could have done over the weekend. Did the boss consider the long-term damage he just did to the loyalty of this VP of sales?

From my experience, mediocre bosses fall into Scenario 1. Great leaders think first, and react second. It is far easier to destroy a team culture than to build one. Scenario 1 is the easy reaction, the one you might have experienced from your boss when you were head of sales (or other functional leader). But if you are going to be a great leader, you ask questions and listen first, and react second. Sounds basic, but fraternity hazing still goes on today for the same reason. It is the old "I had to suffer through it, so they should too". Your ability to break the pattern of bad boss behavior above you will define your ability to become a strong team builder.

Many leaders fail because they never figure out how to become the boss of previous peers. When they were peers, they shared the same issues together, had to produce the same reports, and now they are suddenly telling their previous buddies/peers when that report is due. Others wanted the position you now have, and they are now beneath you. You already won the horse race, you now need to lead to the best of your abilities. You can't worry about being well-liked. Playing basketball at lunch with the factory workers is not considered team building, that just means you like basketball and it allows factory workers to give a hard foul without consequences, since the cultural norms are now basketball norms. You can take your management team to a retreat and do team building exercises, but it will not translate back to the office unless you plan to build a ropes course in the hallway. Setting up informal group breakfasts and lunches with people below you is a good idea if you are prepared to open up. Keep in mind you can be asked some pretty difficult questions, and the real answers may not be appropriate for this level. The meetings are a bust if you are holding back information, as word gets out that the unwritten rule is "small talk" only. The organization will spread the word that real questions will not get answered at the CEO breakfast.

One of the most important aspects of building a healthy team is building a meritocracy. Everyone on the team needs to believe they are on a high performance/reward compensation plan. Go out of your way to create the esprit de corp, the want-to-belong factor that instills internal pride in the worker. Everyone wants to be a part of something. Without that, you will have mercenaries who will jump for the next best offer. You must convey a rah-rah spirit that catches on throughout your company. If you don't build pride, you will eventually lose really good people. You will lose them anyway if they are really good, because everyone is striving for a GM position. If you believe you can keep an A player happy in the role of functional leader forever, you are in for a big disappointment. If you are working at a F500, the whole company should be built around career development to get the stars promoted to the next level up. What happens if you run a $50MM business and you are CEO and president? Your functional leaders have nowhere to go unless your growth is off the charts, creating new divisions and thus new division GM opportunities.

Your goal is to create a senior management team that can run the business if you are not there. The business must be able to run independently with your team. You act as a coach, mentor, and visionary. Identify the best people in your company and continuously challenge and promote them. Make sure they have the key roles. Great managers build outstanding teams who will perform. If you don't have the talent on the inside, go outside and hire the talent. Everyone knows you must conduct references on an individual before they join your company. Make sure each person is the right fit for your team (in addition to being a star) before bringing them on. Reference the culture and style fit as much as the performance. Lots of great performers in one company fail in the next one because the cultural fit is not there. I once recruited the head of human resources from a financial services firm, and he was a star in the fast-paced world of investment banking. He then joined an insurance company that was collegial, team-oriented and slower paced, where the culture quickly rejected him. The style fit was not there.

The best leaders readily hand out compliments and constantly praise top performers. They are also objective as well, and recognize when a person is not contributing their share of the work. Don't wait too long to remove them. It will only hurt your business and the morale of the team.

I often interview the senior management team of a company, all the direct reports to a CEO. In one particular company, all of the direct reports felt very secure in their jobs, and no one felt their job was at risk. The problem is that they weren't all stars, yet they all felt the same level of comfort. In general, 25% should be praised as stars, 25% as highly capable, 25% under Intensive Care (meaning their performance must dramatically improve or they will be pushed out), 15% are in transition (they are still too new in their role for you to know), and 10% should be let go.

If you turn people over frequently in the company, you will spend too much time training and indoctrinating new employees. A strong team builder has low turn-over, which contributes to bigger margins. You must have a team that gels together. If it is all superstars, but each acts as a lone ranger, each will try to win at the expense of the others. In a "Cowboy Culture" everyone is on their own, and everyone else is the enemy. In a "Collegiality Culture", everyone operates in the best interest of the company at all times, and each team member goes out of his/her way to help each other. Certain industries are geared to a Cowboy culture, and other industries are geared to a Collegial one. Investment banking can choose more of a Cowboy culture than a manufacturing company. If a not-for-profit does not have a high Collegial culture, something is really wrong. In the middle is the norm, which means you have landed somewhere in between the two extremes. If you hire a "Cowboy" or a "Collegial" into a middle norm culture, the organization rejects the "Cowboy" and the "Collegial" leaves due to unhappiness. Think about the team culture you have today, and seek honest feedback from your direct reports to understand whether you are leading Cowboy, Collegial, or something in between. You must know what you have before you can decide what you want it to become. And you can't hire for fit if you don't know what your culture is today. The organization structure must match the culture and your management style. Once those are synchronized, you can accurately convey to an outside hire what you are offering and assess the fit.

Part of building your team is hiring the right people. Don't forget to court the outside hire, to pursue them, to make them feel wanted. You are selling if you know they are good, and you should not be in discussions with the person unless you already know they are a star. The Bulls and Knicks recently pursued the same basketball coach at the same time. Both organizations wanted to hire him. He chose the Knicks because "they pursued me, they made me feel like they wanted me. It's nice to feel wanted". Many leaders treat outside candidates like applicants and never land the top talent.

Decision Maker/Risk Taker

WHEN THE TOP consulting firms interview MBAs at the top business schools, the consulting firms commonly ask the MBAs to read a case study during the interview to test the candidate's strategic decision making ability. While this focuses on the intellect side of leadership, no one has a way to test how someone will make decisions when they are running a company.

Taking the wrong path with a business is a sure way to get fired. If you make the wrong decisions, you lose money. Lose money, get fired. It is amazing to me how many leaders fail to correlate their past bad decisions with why they were pushed out by a boss or a Board. I do the informal references and learn that a CEO decided to invest heavily in bricks and mortar expansion and it did not pay off. The CEO was fired for failing to earn a decent return on the investment of fast expansion of multiple retail outlets. If you decide to spend the company's money, everyone is looking for a return on that investment in a specific time frame. If you fail to achieve this return, you made a bad decision and you will be fired as the result. Now you either learn from the mistake as you go forward, or you are just a bad decision maker. Not everyone can learn from their mistakes. I am amazed at how many failed leaders are unable to articulate why or how they failed. Who would put a person in their next leadership role if that person has no idea why they failed in their last position?

There are multiple ways to make decisions. A common path is to get input from each of your direct reports, so you hear "pros and cons" from different functional points of view. Time for you to lead, which means decide which way the company is going to go. Along the way, you have thanked everyone for their input, evolved it to a group decision and created buy-in from everyone along the way, by complimenting their input analysis. If you are constantly making the wrong decision, get out of a leadership role and go back to the functional level where you were successful.

The ability to know <u>when</u> to make a decision is a critical leadership trait. There is no such thing as ever having all the information. Being decisive means knowing when to make a decision and not looking back after you make it (at least not for the next day). Some decisions are made with 10% of available information, others are made with 90% of the information. Sometimes you have no idea how much information is out there.

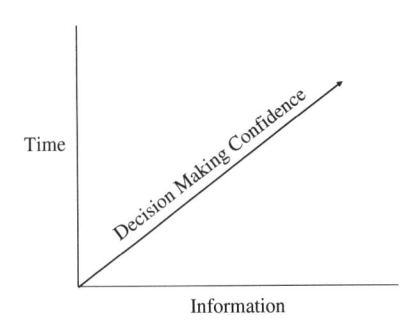

The key is to make a timely decision because you believe you have enough information to pull the trigger.

[Graph: Time vs Information, with diagonal line labeled "Decision Making Confidence"]

If you take too much time, then you have lost your chance to be decisive.

There are 6 versions of the famous "Ready, Aim Fire" decision-making sequence. "Ready" means collecting information. "Aim" means talking to others about the decision you are about to make, to bounce it off them, either to test the way you are leaning or to politically smooth the acceptance of the decision. Aim is gaining group consensus. "Fire" is the announcement of the decision you made.

1.) Ready, Aim, Fire. – The scenario where you have the time to gather 80% of the information, and you have time to trial balloon your decision with others to "test drive" the decision. You have time to build group consensus. This is the optimal decision process, with the highest likelihood of success. It also takes the most time.

2.) Ready, Fire, Aim. – You had time to gather information but did not have the time (or interest) to share the decision with others to get group input. You received feedback after the decision was made.

3.) Aim, Ready, Fire. – You shared your decision with others to get buy-in before gathering information to support it. You want "buy-in" above all else.

4.) Aim, Fire, Ready. – You are trying to defend/support the decision with data (information). Since the decision is already made, there is pressure to skew the data to support the decision.

5.) and 6.) Fire, Aim, Ready/Fire, Ready, Aim. – You made a quick gut call and are now trying to support your judgment with information and support from others. You now want to validate your decision with data and group support. This creates a heavy political environment, as everyone knows you made the call on your own but now want "troop support."

You are going to make some bad decisions, and if you bet wrong on a big one you may have just bet the company as well as your tenure with the company. But you can't take risks if you are not bold. So how do you balance decision making with risk taking? You need to know when to gain group consensus versus make autonomous decisions. You can trust your gut only if you have a history of your gut being right. Know when to admit a wrong decision, and don't be afraid to try and correct it. As you contemplate a tough decision, never walk out to the end of the "diving board" and look down. When you go, run off the end of the board and look straight ahead. Everyone will follow your lead. If you look like you are second guessing a decision, you will quickly lose everyone's confidence.

All good leaders are decisive. You must step in and take a stand. If you are indecisive, you will achieve mediocre performance at best. Employees smell indecisiveness like sharks smell blood. You are paid the big bucks to make the tough decisions. If you bet right on the "company crushing issues" you will be viewed as a very strong leader. If you are wrong often, you may be one level above your comfort zone. If you make too many wrong decisions, life will not be fun. You will be replaced, and you will not have the foresight to remove yourself. No one is objective enough to blame themselves. Over 23 years in search, I have heard every excuse in the book, but rarely "I made the wrong decision." Human nature says you blame others or the circumstances. It is the ability to weather a storm, get back up off the floor, get back on the horse, all those things are part of the make-up of a strong leader. If you are in over your head, drop back to your functional strength, the one you climbed to get to the top. The key is to assess yourself, and be honest about finding examples in your career where you made the right call. If you cannot find examples in your past, you are better suited for consensus decision making. The larger the corporation, the more your decision must be politically validated by the rest of the senior management team and/or anyone above you.

Great decision makers are great CEOs. The press does not understand that a CEO who can dominate an industry is the equivalent of hiring a great quarterback to win the Super Bowl. Are good quarterbacks also great leaders? In the industry called football, they sure are. But I would never think a quarterback could run a business until he proved he could do it. There is no guarantee that leadership transfers across industries. Sticking with the football analogy, no one is going to assume that the ability of a quarterback to read a defense is going to translate into his ability to read a balance sheet. But some people believe that a leader in a tech industry can become a great leader in the grocery business, or a great leader in the paper industry can become a great leader in the software industry. A Board takes a lot of risk recruiting a CEO from one industry to another. The reason is that no one knows how much learning curve time the business will tolerate, nor how much learning curve time the CEO will require. There are lots of examples where the CEO ran out of time before he could make a positive impact. As technology speeds up the world, it speeds up (reduces) the "grace period" of a new CEO, and shrinks their time to make decisions.

Great decision makers can and should command great compensation packages, just like great pro athletes are paid far more than average pro athletes. Let's look at executive pay packages. The media, the public, the analysts, all are screaming to rein in executive pay for CEOs. Why are they screaming? Because they don't understand how hard it is find a truly great leader with a proven track record of making the right decisions. We still live in a free market economy and the cost of a great CEO is established by the market. Many people think it is an arbitrary number set by corporate Boards protecting their buddy. The reality is that if you cut the compensation package in half for a top CEO role, you get to look at CEO candidates who are only half as good as the stars for that sized company in that industry. So let's say a F100 corporation decides to hire an unproven CEO because he costs half as much as the proven ones. And let's say he makes a couple big mistakes and the stock price slides by 50%. Now all the shareholders are irate that their stock value has been cut in half. Will they turn around and say "Well, we all knew we took a calculated risk on paying half what we needed to pay to get a top talent, and we made a bad decision." I don't think so. There would be an absolute failure to realize that "you get what you pay for" in the marketplace. The more proven the leadership talent, the more expensive it is to hire that person. We live in a meritocracy, not a socialistic society where performance is neutralized.

Americans are very comfortable being ranked. In public school in the 1970s, many of us were ranked in elementary school into color-coded reading groups based on reading performance. Brown was the bottom, blue was the top, with many colors in between. America was not afraid to administer weekly reading tests to rank each student. It also provided an incentive to progress, to get to the next level. Of course the program (I think it was called SRA) has been abolished as politically incorrect. As a country, we keep leaning away from rank ordering based on performance. But that is exactly what happens in the business world. You rank order your direct reports, formally and informally. The pyramid is in place at every company. So why do so many people not understand that the person who reached the top of the pyramid is indeed a better performer than the ones who were pushed out of the company three levels back? We should not be afraid to rank order. What are colleges doing when they ask for your grades, SAT/ACT, etc? They are rank ordering the applicant pool. "Pay for performance" is in place for athletes and entertainers, and it needs to stay in place for decision makers in the business world. A great example of decision making occurs around your ability to promote stars, help develop the employee with potential, and fire the underperformer. You must move fast on people, making an early call on non-performers and getting them out of their positions. Equally important is being decisive about who your stars are, praising the stars so you do not lose them.

The internet boom and bust exposed a lot of courage. If you bet big and got in early, you had the opportunity to get out before the bust. If you were a follower and you came in after it was established and had the fear of missing the boat, (meaning you had to see how other companies did first) you probably got caught in the bust. If you did not jump in because you believed it was a fad, you had no upside and no downside.

A CEO's ability to take the right level of risk for the industry you are in is critical. One of the fallacies of leadership is that good leaders have multiple plans in advance. I have heard the theory that Plan A often never happens, so you will need plans B, C, and D already thought out. You better be right more often than wrong on Plan A. If you are right, all the time spent on plans B, C & D was wasted. By the time you see whether Plan A is right or wrong, the competitive landscape has changed enough that plans B, C & D, are probably no longer valid and need to be rethought as well. Better to flex Plan A along the way to implementation to make sure it's right, than to develop B, C & D, which essentially admits up front that you believe you have a 25% chance of being wrong in the beginning.

When you make a decision, you place a business bet. You learn from experience, from betting right and betting wrong. Strong leaders learn something every time they make a bet. It takes courage to take risk, but sometimes it takes more courage to wait, to be patient, to see how the market plays out. That is a decision in itself, to let others go first. There is a thin line between taking intelligent risk and foolhardy risk. A CEO must figure out where the "thin red line" is in his company. If he miscalculates the line, he can put the company out of business, just like taking an army into the wrong battle. CEOs get fired every day for making the wrong decision 12–24 months earlier. It takes a while for the decision to manifest itself in most cases, unless you run a trading firm on Wall Street. Good leaders are right 75% of the time. Great leaders are right 90% of the time. If you are right only 50%

of the time, you won't last, and plans B, C, D will not save you. There is not a lot of time in the rapidly evolving market today, it requires risk-taking with speed.

If your industry is growing and your company is growing, don't screw it up by taking a big risk unless you want to go out on a limb. If your industry is soft and everyone is struggling, you better take some risk on new services/new products or you won't be around for long anyway. Your risk appetite needs to fit your situation. In a multi-billion dollar business, you are steering the super tanker. In a $50MM business, you have a speed boat on your hands. The above advice still holds true for both sized companies.

Prioritization Skills

In 1992, we all witnessed President George Bush lose a reelection to President Bill Clinton, because Bush failed to keep the domestic economy as the centerpiece of his reelection campaign. The Clinton campaign capitalized on it and publicly launched the quote "It's the economy, stupid." Leaders fail when they don't keep "first things first." You must recognize what the overriding statement should be for your current leadership role, and reinforce it at every applicable moment. There isn't always an obvious one, and trying to come up with one can be a dramatic oversimplification for your business. But don't miss it if there is one, and make sure it is meaningful.

One F500 CEO had the habit of repeating a phrase so often that it became the butt of a joke. And once your phrase is used for humor, your respect is undermined every time you use the phrase. Every phrase or culture has a lifespan, just like a restaurant. Very few restaurants stay "hot" for an extended period of time and successfully make the transition to an established restaurant destination in spite of no longer being "hot." And so it is with your number one priority expressed as a statement – you must keep clarifying it to keep it fresh, or it will become as stale as a once-hot restaurant.

Avoid cultural gimmicks, they will backfire on you over time and it is hard to get rid of them. One example is a professional services firm that adopted an aggressive animal as its cultural icon. It worked great during the high growth years, but then you can't get rid of it and it becomes hokey when the growth slows. Small companies can do whatever they want, but be careful because the icon that worked when you were small will become the butt of many jokes as you become larger. Make sure you start phasing it out as soon as cynicism enters the picture.

Following is an example of a F500 company (Company A) where the leader failed to properly focus on the number one priority. Company A had a stagnant stock price and the analysts were screaming for cost cutting. But the CEO was convinced he/she could turn the company around by boosting the revenue side via new products. He believed he could "grow" his way out of the margin issue versus cut costs. He has now made a prioritization gamble. In this case, the CEO bet wrong, as the company failed to market its way out of trouble. The result: termination. This CEO had previously risen through the marketing function to the CEO role, and continued to run the business the same way, from a marketing perspective. Sometimes you believe in the system because the system worked for you. It was the system that enabled you to get to the top. But the system changes as well, and you are in charge of changing the system once you are the CEO. The Board and outside analysts were calling for change. They wanted a much leaner, faster corporation with a focus on operational efficiencies. You give them more of what they had before and you lost your job, the result of a failure to prioritize properly.

So this same Company A now hires CEO #2, and the new CEO comes on board and quickly and effectively addresses the cost side. But the analysts expected that, and 12 months later they are now harping for blockbuster new products. The CEO executes the cost cutting but now fails to reprioritize the company around new product introductions. The analysts scream "Where are the new products?" and the CEO says "Look at my cost cutting measures!" The analysts replied "Yes, you did what you were supposed to do, and that was expected. We rewarded your stock price for the cost-cutting. Now we are going to expect revenue growth via new products while the cost-cutting you put in place protects the new higher margins." The CEO does not get the message, and rides a year on cost-cutting. The result: termination. So the same Company A then hires CEO #3, who has a great track record of new product introductions. CEO #1 and CEO #2 both failed to reprioritize the company on a timely basis and it cost them their jobs. Time will tell if CEO #3 will be successful, but the priority is very clear to all. Being CEO is not easy, but that is why you get the big bucks. And all the press who criticize CEO pay, they never ran a company so they have no idea what it takes to be really good.

Let's take F500 Company B as our next example of failing to prioritize. In this case, the CEO set a clear vision and everyone agreed on the top priority, but he then allowed himself to be pulled in multiple directions by different constituencies. He had the right prioritization, but he failed to stick to it. The direct report who made the most recent persuasive pitch to the CEO was able to shift the CEO's thinking, and as a result the company ended up with a "strategy de jour." Result: termination. This particular F500 CEO worried too much about being well-liked instead of leading the company and staying focused.

Successful leaders always have a running priority list of what needs to be done, and they know the rank order. They are highly organized and in-control of what their number one priority should be each day. The key is to constantly prioritize and know what's next. Most leaders use a ritual to get organized. The natural time points are Sunday evening and Monday morning. The right methodology is whatever works for you. Daily "fire-fights" will detract from time spent executing but you cannot let them mentally distract you. As soon as the reactive fire-fight is over, he/she proactively returns to focus on the top of the list.

You must communicate the priorities consistently without overkill (leads to sarcastic cynicism). You must demand the same prioritization and organization skills from your senior management team and make sure they agree with yours. If you have an open forum with your senior management team, you will be able to listen to everyone's best thinking. They will speak their mind without fear of reprisal. If you can create a non-political, open-forum atmosphere, you can get group agreement on the prioritization order from the best minds of the group. You get to make the final call, you are the leader. It is impossible to be bad at prioritization and be viewed as a strong leader. The CEO must constantly communicate and review his prioritization rank order with his check points: Board, direct reports, customers, vendors, shareholders, analyst community (if public), and employees.

Time management skills are critical to leadership. You better be very efficient if you want to lead. If you are disorganized, I don't care how brilliant you might be, you will never be an effective leader. A disorganized strategist should be the head of strategy or work at a top management consulting firm and be a lot happier. Disorganized people waste other people's time, and that is the opposite of what you are supposed to be as a leader.

Business Intelligence

As a recruiter, one of the first things you learn about interviewing people is to ignore the education degrees on their resume. You learn that a top school does not necessarily correlate to top leadership skills. The facts are that more CEOs come from state funded undergraduate colleges and universities than from all the private schools, Ivy League included. If you want to go into investment banking or consulting, that is different; the school you attend is an early intelligence screen for both those industries.

I define Business Intelligence as a blend of Raw Intelligence (RI) which equates to IQ; Emotional Intelligence (EI) which equates to emotional maturity; Street Intelligence (SI) which equates to "street smarts"; and Strategic Intelligence (Strat I) which equates to understanding business frameworks. It's great if you score high across all 4, but it's not required. There was a list in the mid 1980s of the

"10 Toughest Bosses," the ones who went on tirades, yelled, screamed, pounded on the desk, etc. Those bosses were all low on Emotional Intelligence. EI weighs heavily in terms of how you manage people. Low EI will cause you to constantly lose all your good people, and can cause bad decision making. For example, with low Emotional Intelligence you might decide on the wrong strategic decision because you need to prove that someone else is wrong, versus decide what is right for the business. The goal is to be above average across all 4 types of intelligence. You can use strength in one to shore up a neutral in another, and that is what the great leaders tend to do. There are great leaders with average Raw Intelligence, but all successful leaders are strong in at least one of the four intelligence categories. It is amazing to me how far a CEO can get with only one of the 4 Intelligence traits as a strength, as long as the other three are neutral versus weaknesses.

Part of Emotional Intelligence is a measure of a CEO's self-awareness as it relates to people. High EI means you have a natural style and ability to communicate with all levels in the organization. Employees at all levels naturally like you. Leaders without high Emotional Intelligence tend to be viewed as aloof, stand-offish, moody, egocentric or temperamental.

If your Raw Intelligence is high, you usually possess a great memory capacity with high attention to detail. Others in the company will claim you have a photographic memory. If you don't have high RI, you will need to be much more organized to compensate for it. High attention to detail is critical for all leaders. As the size of the organization goes up, the definition of what constitutes a "detail" goes up with it, but the ability must still be there.

Too much Strategic Intelligence can lead to inertia. I have seen ineffective leaders with very high SI. Their downfall is often caused by over-thinking a situation, (analysis paralysis), high frustration over no one else being on their same mental plane and speed, and a failure to keep it simple. Too little Strategic Intelligence is also a problem. If you can't keep pace intellectually with your direct reports, you lose their respect quickly. If you focus too much on tactics, those below you will question why you are leading them, especially if they are the ones always coming up with the strategic direction.

The key is to match your intelligence levels to the right industry. You better be high on Raw (RI) and Strategic (Strat I) if you are going to lead in a complex technology industry that is evolving everyday. And you better be high on Emotional (EI) if you are going to lead a service firm like consulting, law, etc. Many leaders fail because their intelligence levels are not matched well with their industry. Ask your closest friends how they would rank the 4 intelligences for you, which is first, second, third and fourth? If they all pick a clear first, and that is different than the demands of your current job/industry, you need to make a change before the change is made for you. A top MBA program does a great job of helping you select your best industry fit. If you are struggling to keep up with the best classmates in finance, why would you pursue investment banking? If you are just ok in accounting, surely that would steer you away from the accounting industry. Likewise, a natural proclivity toward developing relationships should steer you to client/account management.

Over my years of interviewing leaders, I have noticed several patterns: high Emotional and average Raw and Strategic can make a very successful leader of a service firm. High Strategic and high Raw with low Emotional (EI) is better suited for a head of strategy position or management consulting. It is becoming rare to find a successful leader today with low Emotional (EI). Leaders with high Raw and Strategic and low Emotional can survive if they are leading in a highly complex, fast-growing technology industry. An M&A investment banker with off-the-chart quantitative skills can get away with low Emotional (EI) and still have a very successful career, but that person should not become the head of M&A for an office. When Emotional (EI) is low for a leader, it creates an environment where the senior management team does a lot of talking around the CEO, with a lot of manipulation to get the CEO to come up with the decision that everyone else wants. There is the tendency to treat a CEO with low Emotional (EI) with "kid gloves" in hopes of avoiding confrontational behavior.

A high Street Intelligence is manifested as having a "gut feel" for what to do with the business. It usually relates to business decisions based on how people will react to the decision. An example is a well-known sporting goods company that decided to create consumer "pull" versus trade "push" with their products. The CEO underestimated the role of the golf pro in the selling cycle to the consumer. His lack of "street smarts" caused sales to plummet, as the golf pro convinced the consumer to buy a competitor's product.

Commitment and Focus

Focus allows you to learn all the critical details about your business, and to not memorize or dwell on non-critical information. It means not spending mental capacity on anything that is not critical to your business. I often see a CEO who is very committed and focused on the business, but unable to have (or want, I am not sure) a balanced life. I noticed a F500 CEO had part of his house under construction. I asked him who his architect and construction firm were, and he did not know the architect or the builder, his spouse was handling everything. He did not need to add that information to his life, and he trusted his spouse's capabilities to handle it. The downside can be a CEO not knowing the name of his daughter's 4th grade teacher, or not seeing any of his child's soccer games.

Taking on a leadership position, in any capacity, requires commitment. Commitment is a trait that a leader drives throughout the organization and it must be apparent through good and bad times. A leader may be questioned on business decisions along the way, but he/she should never be questioned on his/her commitment. As soon as someone legitimately questions your commitment, they are about to put an arrow in your back.

If your business commitment outweighs everything else, then all personal relationships and interests are moved to the back-burner. It is fine if you choose the one-dimensional life of career over all else, but make sure that anyone you hire has the same commitment. If you are working 65 hours a week, you will definitely fire or cause to leave anyone who works 45 hours a week. Resentment grows on both sides, and you the boss always win. It is very rare for a boss to tolerate a different amount of hours than he/she works. Be very clear how many hours you expect, and don't use the oldest line in the business, "whatever it takes to get the job done." That line only works if the person is on 100% commission. If you are a workaholic, be honest about it. If you are doing it by choice, tell your employees that business is your hobby. This is your chance to change the culture since you are now the leader and the keeper of the culture. If you are single, it is easy to put all your commitment into your company. If family or personal time is critical to you, you must communicate this to others as well. Do not create a double standard. Human nature says you will resent anyone working fewer hours than you are working. On the other hand, "fraternity hazing" is not popular anymore. Making lower level employees work crazy hours "because I did it" will not go over well with the current generation, and you will have fewer employees to choose from.

As soon as you question your own commitment, figure out if you are simply burned out and need a vacation, or if you have truly lost interest and need a change. Some leaders argue that life balance is a requirement, and that you need more than one area of focus in your life. It's not true. I have seen many successful and happy leaders who live to work. Work can be your life, but you better be comfortable with occasional loneliness, since your "friends" disappear on the weekends. If you are a workaholic, everyone will realize that work is everything to you, and they will attempt to hide a balanced life from you.

For example, I know a CEO who works most Saturdays. In his mind, he leads a balanced life and he only occasionally works a Saturday. The reality is that he expects his senior management team to be there every Saturday when he is there. But when he interviews for a direct report position, he never mentions the Saturday requirement. He has a self-perception issue. People perceive themselves differently from reality. Your goal is to close the gap between reality and perception, so that you actually communicate up front to a direct report, "I work 75% of all Saturdays." Then if you only work 50% of them, it's a positive for the new hire versus feeling blind-sided by the sudden realization that most Saturdays are mandatory. If you are Mr. Saturday and hire someone who has life balance, that person will be stressed and shocked when the Saturday surprise hits him/her. The worst illusion is the CEO who works Saturdays but says "you work whenever you need to work," because he doesn't mean it. As a direct report, if you show up Monday and decisions were made on Saturday by the rest of the team, you are in trouble.

On the other side of the coin, many leaders miss the cues of when they need to step up and make a key time commitment decision that affects their life balance. If you are not prepared to make unexpected, unplanned changes to your personal life, you need to decide what level of leadership you are seeking. A great leader understands when to miss the first day of vacation, or when to cancel the vacation all together. A great leader has a 6th sense of when to drop everything to get something done that is critical to the business. Many leaders fail because they do not flex their personal time. They stick with the pre-planned personal trip, and they fail to recognize when they are at a "make or break" decision point for their company. And they suffer for it. If a leader works 40 hours a week and the business dynamics call for 50 hours per week, that leader will fail. Life balance does not mean you won't make a personal sacrifice to do the right thing for the business at a critical point in time. Understand the commitment requirement of the industry and company, and make sure you are ready for that level of commitment. Investment bankers work lots of hours, there is no way around it. You don't go into investment banking or management consulting with the words "life balance" in your vocabulary. As a leader, there will always be times when you need to "drop everything" and tend to a pressing critical business issue. Failure to step up and show the focus and commitment needed in a crunch time will cause a lack of respect from your direct reports. Investment bankers cannot work 40 hours a week, the industry simply won't support it. The time you spend on the business per week depends on the industry, and on your personal goals for the business (cash cow versus invest for growth).

Toughness

I WATCH A LOT of leaders fail because they are simply too nice. They don't have the stomach for the tough people issues, or the tough "make or break" strategic decisions and it leads to their downfall. Great leaders make the tough decisions for the business even though there may be negative ramifications to an individual or a group of employees.

Like a great athlete, good leaders focus on competitors to exploit any weaknesses. Leaders understand but avoid focusing on competitor's strengths, which can cause the athletic term of getting "psyched out". A leader must have the mental toughness to stay focused and not let negative thoughts cloud their ability to lead. An example of a negative thought is "we are never going to make that number." If you really believe you can't make it, bring your analysis to the boss or Board now, because no one likes surprises.

Avoid expressing a negative thought. As soon as a pro golfer thinks about hitting a tee shot out-of-bounds to the left, the odds of hitting the fairway are greatly diminished. It might go hard right as an over-compensation for the negative thought, but you can bet the ball is not going down the middle of the fairway. As soon as the pro tennis player thinks about faulting, the odds of the next serve being a fault just doubled. The same holds true for corporate leadership. Maintain mental toughness to avoid negative thoughts from entering your mind and stay focused on driving the business forward. The ability to apply unwavering focus over the course of a year is an example of mental toughness. A great example of mental toughness is terminating a B-grade employee whom 1.) you like, 2.) does an adequate job, and 3.) is well liked by everyone else in the company. The right decision is to replace the B with an A-level performer, especially if it shows the organization that this is a meritocracy and the stars rise to the top. It could be an unpopular move in the short term, but the failure to do it will paint you as a leader who is afraid to make the unpopular decision. Many leaders deal with a tough decision by going into stall mode. If you are postponing the inevitable, that is a big mistake. Everyone will say, "he/she should have terminated that person 6 months ago."

Stars will respect you for eliminating anyone who is not a star, even if the overall corporate feeling supports the person. You want to create a culture that does not promote B players.

"Physically tough" does not mean the same thing in business as it does if you are a football player. In business, it is the ability to sustain a high level of energy over long periods of time. Part of leading is keeping everyone else energized by setting a great example. Especially when it comes to negotiating with a customer or leading an all day meeting, physical toughness and mental toughness come together. It is easy to think of examples of physical toughness from the sports world. Kirk Gibson of the LA Dodgers hitting a World Series home run with a pulled groin muscle, or Pete Sampras vomiting on the tennis court but holding on to win the U.S. Open. But how do you translate those images of toughness to the business world? Look at former NYC Mayor Rudy Giuliani in the aftermath of 9/11, and his ability to keep going with a high energy level around the clock, day-after-day. As a leader, you can't be the one who runs out of gas at the end of a long day. You need to be the one who steps up and provides the energy to get everyone through the day with an optimistic "glass half full" view of tomorrow.

Let's stay with the Giuliani example. In the NYC 9/11 aftermath, the nation saw Giuliani as a tough leader in the face of unprecedented circumstances. Externally, leaders must present a tough image that seemingly cannot be ruffled. Situational toughness must be a part of any successful leader. You must be tough to successfully lead through a crisis. The true test of toughness is to lead through a period of great challenge. Great leaders keep a level of distance from those they lead in order to make the tough decisions. A leader must show superb resilience. He/she must always display courage and calmness. You cannot appear to be ruffled even if you are scared stiff. You must step in on the tough issue and make the call. You cannot be afraid of fear. You respect it, but you are not afraid of it. You are paid the big bucks to step up in a time of a business crisis. If a major competitor drops their price, the union strikes, the plant is shut down by the FDA, etc, how you lead in a time of crisis at your company will make or break you as a leader. And no employee will forget how you performed under stress, never forget you are always under the microscope.

Too much toughness leads to playing dictator, because you believe you are tough enough to do it all yourself and you fail to properly delegate (the Alexander Haig syndrome). Too little toughness and you will lose the respect of your direct reports, and then you are finished. Toughness does not compete with humaneness, it competes with ambivalence.

Many leaders have failed to remove a weak-performing subordinate in a timely manner and it has cost the leader their job. If they had removed the weak subordinate on a timely basis, they would have made the tough decision. You must step up to decisions on a timely basis versus hope they will go away. Your original instinct will prove itself correct 90% of the time with under-performers if you are good. Everyone else (peers of the person) all know when a person is under-performing, and they (peers) know you haven't done anything about it yet.

Failure to make the tough decision can be a career-limiting mistake that prevents you from moving up. If you are the CEO of a F500 and you lack toughness, it is only a matter of time before the Board removes you. When you feel a difficult decision, wade into it and start getting as much detail as possible. Never appear to be "frozen" versus stalling as a tactic. You will ultimately be viewed as "too soft," or "unable to make the tough calls." Can toughness be improved? Absolutely. It can come with business maturity and with practice. The early lack of toughness in cutting an underperformer can be replaced with a focused toughness to cut the next one on a timely basis. Toughness is not about being mean or cruel, it is about running the business efficiently. Many athletes don't like contact sports early in their career but then grow to embrace the contact as they mature. The same can occur in a leader. You might lose sleep on the person you need to cut if you truly like them, but over time you will not lose sleep as your perspective grows and you realize it is not personal, it is business. If you keep losing sleep on people decisions, you are probably in over your head. You can increase your toughness over time as long as you learn from your mistakes. Dealing with a tough business issue can be a very defining career move for many leaders. Recognizing the difficult decision and forcing the issue to the forefront of the agenda is a hallmark of a tough leader. It is often easier to look the other way and blame another department, function, or person for an issue you clearly saw coming. The easy way out is to let those below you deal with the problem. But stepping up to the issue no one wants to face is the sign of a true leader. Forcing the issue from the back burner to the front of the agenda before it is easily recognized as a problem takes toughness. We are not talking about macho toughness, we are talking about focus and taking on the difficult decisions head-on. Those below you will increase versus decrease their level of respect for you. The higher the level of respect you have with your direct reports and the Board above you, the more leeway you have to eventually make a mistake. And you will make a mistake. So build a cushion for error by excelling at tough decisions and making the right call. The key is to build the cushion as you continue to develop as a well-rounded GM.

One of the hardest moves to make is to suddenly find yourself managing your former peers. I know a CEO who was pushed out by the Board because he was too easy on his senior management team (former peers). He was promoted from those ranks, so he was once a peer of all his current direct reports. This CEO tried to appease too many of his former peers versus stick to his vision and strategy. You must have a tough emotional make-up that does not need coddling or praise. You don't need to be unfriendly, but you can't require being well-liked as part of your disposition. If you are well-liked and respected, you just made it to the top 10% of leaders.

Another F500 CEO changed the culture of a company without improving performance. The CEO got rid of the traditional "Midwestern values" culture in an effort to be leaner, meaner, and faster. But all the CEO did was successfully install "meaner" without leaner or faster. He also failed to create a new vision that would result in higher performance. No one understood where the company was going, but everyone knew it was no longer a nice place to work. The CEO implemented a "tough place to work" culture without improved performance. The Board removed the CEO as soon as one of the star functional leaders resigned from the company.

Part of being tough as a leader is not needing anyone to pat you on the back. You are responsible for patting others on the back, but you must have the resiliency to persevere when no one is there to give you a moral boost at crunch time. Your ability to keep complimenting those around you when no one is there to compliment you is a key part of developing the emotional side of toughness required to be a strong leader. It can be very lonely at the top, which is why many leaders join a peer group on the outside like YPO.

Don't "Widgetize" the Customer

There are lots of business posters focused on the customer. You know the motivational posters, such as the one with a breeching whale or a soaring eagle, and a caption that says: "the most important aspect of this business is how we treat the customer everyday." Everyone knows the customer should be the focus. Your role is to stop your company from viewing customers as part of a business process. Your job is to make everyone in your company believe that the customer needs to be treated like a fire in the woods in the winter. Pretend you are lost in a snow blizzard, and you used your only match to start a fire. If that fire goes out, you will not survive. That is how you need to get your company thinking about the care, feeding, protection, and service of each customer – like they are the link to your company's survival. It is critical to your role as a business leader to know when to walk away from customers as well. You cannot meet all demands and you should not meet low margins. But teach the organization beneath you that when the customer says "Jump," your company responds with "How High?" Otherwise your company will debate whether to jump or not. The whole company will watch to see "how high" you jump, and then mimic your "jump". Many leaders do not realize they set the standard for how customers are viewed and treated by the entire organization.

As the leader, you must ensure that the company does not "widgetize" your customers. It is easy to lose perspective of the individual characteristics of your customers. If you are out of the day-to-day customer loop, you will start to assume that you understand your customers' needs and begin to "widgetize" them. Over time, it is easy to accidentally stop treating them as individuals, and instead, treat them like part of a business process. Guess how customers feel when they sense they are part of a business process? They feel like trying someone else's service or product.

How do you stay involved with customers if you are the leader? Figure out what level of customer contact your industry requires, every industry is different. The key is to create formal processes around customer feedback, and make sure you get copied on the good and the bad. The only way it works is if the feedback is confidential, otherwise no customer will say what they actually think. Don't be afraid to attempt to lead your company to a higher value-added level of customer interaction. Many leaders have helped a company evolve from the backslapping, boozing days of customer entertainment to the value-added focus that benefits both sides. As the leader, you set the tone for everyone else on how you view customers, treat customers, and interact with customers. How you talk about customers will be mimicked throughout the organization. Many leaders pay lip service to a customer focus but in reality view customers as an accounts-receivable headache. Think about the bumper sticker styled message that reads "this would be a great business if it weren't for the customers." If you talk about customers in the company like they are a thorn in your side, everyone in the company will view customers the same way and eventually the customers will figure out that is exactly how they are being viewed by your company.

Let's assume you deliver a high quality good or service on time. Easy to keep customers, right? Wrong. If you don't make them feel good, you will still lose them. Here's the great coincidence – the same holds true with how you treat your own people. Even if you pay them at or above market rates, if you don't make them feel good, you will lose your stars. Can you get a customer back after losing them? Yes, just like you can sometimes stop a resignation by telling that person how much the company really does value that person. In other words, you've got to make them feel wanted. You can sometimes get a customer back, and you can sometimes reverse a resignation by letting that person know how important they really are to the organization. One CEO was trying to "partner" (that means sell) to a F100 that had created a very demanding set of rules for "partnership" with vendors. This vendor finally realized that being a "partner" meant selling their products at close to cost to this F100 company. The problem is that if you treat your vendors poorly, you will eventually also treat your customers poorly. The organization will have trouble being a ruthless cost squeezer to vendors, and a relationship building "feel good" company to customers. You must create some form of a "customer appreciation day" to make it evident to the organization that your company cares a lot about customers. This gets tough when you have two tiers of customers. Take the consumer packaged goods industry: your customer is the retail grocery channel that sells your products, and your customer is the consumer. You now have two different sets of customers with very different needs. And the easy thing to do is start treating the grocery channel like a necessary evil instead of a customer. Your job is to reinforce to the organization that both are the customer. Don't call grocery retailers "the trade", call them customers, that is what they are! A sporting goods company once tried to market and advertise directly to the consumer to force "the channel" (pro shops) to carry their products. It did not work, because "the trade" switched every consumer who walked in the door to someone else's products, someone who made them feel important as a customer (and "spiffed" (increased) them on their sales commission). Don't let your organization call a customer (someone who buys your product or service) names such as "the trade", "the channel", "the distributor", etc., or you will eventually lose them as customers. You get one chance to shift the paradigm of perception on a multi-tiered customer business, do not miss your window of opportunity.

Creates vs. Facilitates Process

WHEN YOU BECOME a leader for the first time, you now have the right to assess the business processes in place. The larger the organization, the more complex the processes become, and the greater opportunity for bureaucracy, duplication and inefficiencies. A leader is in the position to evaluate the processes necessary to run the business and get rid of the excess. Many good leaders of Fortune 500 companies are hired for their ability to facilitate processes, not create them. Of course everyone should strive to eliminate bureaucracy and slow decision making. If your company wants you to create processes and you don't do it, you will fail. If all the processes work well in the company and your job is to increase sales/profitability through the existing processes, you will fail if you spend time changing the existing processes. A great process facilitator ensures that the top performers are benefiting from existing processes in place. You are going to be personally better suited for the ability to either create or facilitate, because to excel at both is rare.

In most businesses, the business processes have become bureaucratic hurdles to efficiency. That means all your best people must find ways to work around the existing processes. Your job is to help them stop wasting their time. You must create an open dialogue and learn which processes are being circumvented, and then get rid of those processes.

The people you hire as your business grows should also be identified as process creators or process facilitators. You must know the core processes and how effectively the processes are working. When processes don't work, that is when the "evil twins" (sarcasm and cynicism), creep into the organization. For example, think back to pre 9/11 days. If you worked in a large commercial office building, think about how you felt when you were required to sign out of a building when you left to go home at night. In most commercial office buildings across America, you were asked to stand in a line and sign out. The nonsense of this exercise, which was repeated across corporate America every night, was highlighted by the fact that you were not required to sign in when you entered the building if you arrived before 8.a.m. A form of i.d. was not required upon signing out, so you could write any name you wanted in the sign-out book. So the sarcasm and cynicism came in, and the sign-out ledger book always contained names like Donald Duck and Mickey Mouse.

Great example of a meaningless process that wasted people's time.

If you are the leader, you are responsible for getting rid of processes that waste people's time and do not add value. It does not matter how long a process has been in place, get rid of it! As the leader, you must keep a pulse on how to make processes more effective and recognize when a process has become too bureaucratic and is now an impediment to growth. As soon as you hear the words "that is how we have always done it," you know two things. First, the person speaking is not a thinker, the person is reactive versus proactive. Secondly, you have come across a bureaucratic process that needs evaluation.

If you are going to start a new business or a division, you better be a process creator versus a process facilitator. As a F500 CEO, you are a process facilitator by the nature of the size of the business, and you are turning the wheel of a cruise ship versus a powerboat. If you are a process creator, do not aspire to lead a F500 corporation. If you are a process facilitator, do not aspire to step out from the F500 and join a private-equity backed portfolio company with $50MM in revenue. Both scenarios will have a high likelihood of failure. When you hear people talk about why people fail, I often hear words that relate to being on the wrong side of the process fit. Following is a translation of informal reference comments on why various CEOs failed:

"Didn't get anything done" – A process facilitator in a process creator environment.

"Bull in a china shop" – A process creator in a process facilitator environment.

"Not hands-on, lack of details on the business, could not make good decisions" – A process facilitator stuck in a process creator environment.

"Stayed at 1,000 feet" – A process facilitator stays above the detail, a process creator works on the ground.

"Too hands-on" – A micromanager (process creator) unable to move up to 1,000 feet, unable to work in a process facilitator role.

In summary, process creators should not lead F500 companies, and process facilitators should not try to go lead small private-equity backed companies. Both will fail. Figure out which one you are and match that to the size of the company to enhance your success.

Know Your Numbers

EVERY GREAT LEADER tears his numbers apart to understand the business and then rebuilds them, line item by line item. You must first break down every input variable and know exactly what is behind every number. This ensures one of the key financial leadership tenets: the numbers can never mislead you, and you can never be humiliated by anyone who asks you what is behind a specific number. Get rid of any numbers that don't make sense to you. Change the financials until you have your personal stamp on what is reported when. Get a CFO whom you trust so you are never embarrassed and never without an explanation of what the numbers mean. Most importantly, the integrity level of your CFO must match your integrity level, so that the CFO is never leading the effort to push the envelope. Your job is to set the integrity bar and expect your CFO to stay above it. You want your CFO to say "I think that is stretching the envelope and we should not do it," versus your CFO proactively saying "I can hide revenue into the next year if you need me to."

Strong leaders break down all their financials for the same reason we still teach the fundamentals of math in our schools. Why teach math versus teach how to use a calculator? The answer lies in applying the learning. Many leaders fail because they lack a thorough understanding of what the numbers are telling them. You can't hold people accountable if you don't have accurate numbers. Involve your CFO and finance team in the process with you, so you form a partnership that cannot be broken and is based on mutual trust. If you cannot get comfortable with the numbers, you should not try to lead as a general manager. Many great leaders do not have financial backgrounds, but all strong leaders are financially adept and understand their numbers. You cannot develop a feel for the rhythm and cycles of your business unless you have "hard" numbers delivered consistently on time. No leader can run a business without understanding the numbers, and you must have a trusted finance team to know you are seeing accurate, timely numbers. Every good leader develops a 6th sense for the business based on the numbers. They see the trends, and they can extrapolate what is occurring on the operating side from the numbers. This financial instinct is a requirement for success. You will fail without it.

If it comes naturally to you, then the numbers form natural patterns for you. Like driving a car to a new destination, some people do not need to consciously memorize the way back because their mind takes a picture of the return trip. If your financial skills are such that your mind forms business operating patterns from the numbers, you will not need to exert a lot of effort to be able to interpret the numbers. If you are like most, you will need to work hard at deciphering the numbers and learning the implications of various trends and patterns. Work at it until the numbers form business patterns and trends for you.

If you look back at the multiple fraud scandals, the CFO was almost always indicted with the CEO. You must form a great partnership with your CFO, but you are leading the CFO, never vice versa. You must be able to challenge your CFO and his numbers at anytime, and that action should not cause stress in the relationship. Every CEO has options and choices on how creative they want to be with the balance sheet and income statement. Many private equity backed company CEOs try to create a "rainy day fund" where they can "park" some revenue or earnings in case they hit an unexpected bump in the road. We are not talking fraud here, we are talking about under-reporting to leave some room for error if sales get soft at the end of the year. Clearly your CFO must be in collaboration on this common move. A surprise on the upside results in larger bonuses and cigar dinners; a surprise on the downside (when you said you would make the numbers and you didn't) can result in termination.

The "rainy day fund" or "reserve" is a slippery slope, one that already involves a rationalization on why it is ok to withhold some information and revenue. It sends a message to the CFO that creativity is going to be rewarded, and gets his/her mind going in the direction of creativity, a dangerous place to go for a CFO. Keep it clean and make it or break it on straight up numbers, it will pay off in the long run, even if it hurts you in the short term. Remember, backdating options might have started as an idea to provide an effective counteroffer to keep a star from leaving your company.

Adaptability

AN INDUSTRY HAS a pattern, a cycle time, a rhythm, it's own flow. An industry also fits a certain leadership style. It's why your personal industry fit really *does* matter. Jack Welch had to pick from four division presidents to choose his successor. He picked Jeff Immelt and the other three left for new industries. I don't think any of the other three are in those jobs today. You cannot underestimate how different one industry is from the next. The faster you can adapt, the more flexibility and options you have regarding the number of different industries where you can be successful. If you are a slow adapter, never venture outside your own industry because you will fail. Every time a leader steps into a new industry, he/she only has a certain amount of time before the "honeymoon" grace period is over. Some industries have an extremely complex macro competitive situation on their hands (e.g. wireless telecom) and a new leader has very little time to come up to speed. If you need 6 months, you could be fired and the business will be in trouble. Would you take a stereotypical football coach (win at all costs) and put him in a government contracts business? Most likely, he will foster a culture of kickbacks (pun intended) to ensure he wins. Does an industrial manufacturing leadership style fit in a consumer packaged goods company? Can a financial services CEO lead an industrial company? The industry rhythms are all completely different.

How much time do you have to learn a new industry? It depends on how much of a quick study you are, how fast you learn, how adaptable you are. The landscape is littered with failed CEOs who underestimated the learning curve of a new industry. You better be very smart to jump into a complicated technology landscape today, as it is changing so fast there is no learning curve time.

To be a successful leader, you must be comfortable embracing ambiguity. You must be able to take a complex ambiguous situation and simplify it to move to a solution. Even if you are unsure, you must have a plan, and you must communicate that plan. The key is to ask successful veterans about an industry. How fast can an outsider learn it? Gather enough data points to know how much time you will have, and decide if you are faster or slower than the norm. Find the industry that matches your strengths, then find the company within the industry that matches your strengths. How do you measure your adaptability level? Listen to others describe a stressful situation in their lives. If it sounds routine to you, there is a good chance your adaptability factor is high. If you marvel at the adaptability of others, you know you need to avoid change. The formula for adaptability is first based on intelligence. How quickly you comprehend all the drivers and nuances of a new industry has a lot to do with how smart you are. Next is how hard you work, meaning how much time you put in to learn the new business. How much information do you retain the first time you are exposed to new information?

Many CEOs have moved from one F500 industry to another and failed miserably because they were not fast enough to adapt. Another barrier to adaptability is ego. Ego allows a leader to believe that one can learn any new industry. That might be true, given an unlimited amount of time. There is a reason that all the school aptitude tests are timed. Many can figure out the right answer to a problem over an indefinite amount of time, but then you would not have nearly as much differentiation among the test takers. The same is true with jumping into a new company or new industry. If you are good, you will eventually figure out how to be successful running it. But how much time will it take you to be good, and how much time do you have? If you grow up in one industry, you have no idea how long it took you to learn it. The executive search industry is littered with stories of placing high-profile CEOs who were stars in their last industry, but failed by jumping industries. They didn't stop being good, they ran out of time before they could prove they were good in the new environment.

So the first question is to ask yourself how much time you need to learn the industry, and then figure out if that matches with how much time you are being given. Figure out who holds the clock. Is it the analysts, the Board, your boss, top customers, a private equity firm, who has the clock? If you will need twelve months to learn a new industry, be aware that no one will give you that much time from the outside.

To use a sports analogy, we play paddle tennis in Chicago. The court is elevated and is a half-sized tennis court surrounded by chicken wire, which allows for play off the screens. It takes really good Division 1 tennis players around 3 years to really learn the sport. For example, the national doubles champs in paddle tennis could invite any top world tennis doubles team and crush them in a paddle match. In fact, the best tennis doubles team in the world would lose to a top 10 nationally ranked paddle team until they learned the game. The same is true in business. What looks like a lot of analogous variables will be different enough to cause you to fail if you don't have time to learn the nuances.

Innovator/Creator

How do you lead innovation in a company? You must be willing to take risks and spend money. There are multiple F500 CEOs who have zero personal creativity, yet they are willing to spend on creating an innovative culture, or buy innovative ideas from the outside. The toughest part about creativity is pulling back from the non-stop focus on making the day-to-day numbers. Every leader becomes absorbed in the line management of the business, which is what you have been taught to do. It is extremely difficult to change a culture and suddenly have everyone pour creativity into the hallways. The more likely scenario is to make sure there is a small group, a swat team, whose sole purpose is to come up with Big Ideas. Your job is to figure out which key ideas should reach the market. Often times a company has great ideas, but no means to get the idea into the market on a timely basis. You must either empower someone with a budget to take risk and test new ideas, or you need to personally pick great ideas and put them into the market.

One F100 CEO realized that every great product idea introduced in their industry in the past 10 years was sitting in a research notebook in their own company, but a competitor always introduced the new product to market. If your corporate culture is leaving all the innovative new product ideas on the shelf, the outside world will blame you. So find a source for creative ideas and get some new products/services out there to test them, or lose your job due to lack of revenue growth caused by a lack of new product introductions. Your job is to figure out if a bureaucratic process is stopping innovation, or you the leader is preventing it from happening.

Innovation costs money. The old "catch 22" kicks in, meaning if your earnings are too low to justify any extra spending, you stop spending on new products. And you can't increase revenue because you don't have any new products. So how do strong leaders deal with the issue? First, they hire outside firms to pick the next trend or discover the next unrecognized need. None of us knew we needed to pay $3.75 for our coffee when we were spending .50☐ for coffee, but Starbucks created a product around an unrecognized need. You must be willing to spend on market research, engineering, trend-pickers, macro soothsayers, new product development, to put a product or service out there. P&G has great success with Swiffer, a new "dry" cleaning product. P&G decided to focus on bathroom cleaning as a category, and then they hired an outside firm to develop new product concepts, like dry static cleaning. They did not create the idea in-house. If you can grow it in-house, more power to you. If you don't have an inside group and you won't spend on outside research, why would you expect new products?

Lots of companies with bureaucratic, staid cultures are labeled as being "innovative" because they introduced a successful new product. Sometimes it is simply a matter of the leader taking risk and making a key decision to push a product from idea stage to market. You are paid the big bucks to take some risk, so take some. I asked one F500 CEO what he thought of marketing research, and his answer was "it is useful for me to use it as political support after I have a new idea." What's clear is that no one will spend time on innovation or great ideas if they are not rewarded to do so. Say you foster an environment where the head of innovation creates virtual teams across the company to do white board brainstorm sessions. What is each team member's incentive to spend time away from the core business, unless it somehow is expected/demanded in the culture, or rewarded?

Some of the companies that have received innovation awards feel like bureaucratic molasses once you are inside them. You can't imagine how someone could get an innovative idea to the market. The answer is the leader. At some point, the CEO pointed to an idea, made a decision, and assigned responsibility to launch the product. And that is why the product went out the door. You must either create the new product process (process creator) in your company to make sure innovative ideas are coming to your attention, or you need to personally direct some new product efforts. I see many F500 companies that have a lot of pressure to create innovative new products and are unable to do so, because the leader at the top is unwilling to change the existing culture that stymies new product development. And he/she is unwilling to take the personal risk. So as a result, no new products (beyond line extensions) go out the door.

Look at the pharma industry. These companies must constantly pump out the next billion dollar blockbuster product or their stock will drop. The reality is that you could have a non-existent innovation culture, but hire a great team of R&D lab chemists and tell them to create the next wonder drug. If they are successful, your company will be hailed as a great innovator. So there are lots of ways to take innovation/new product risk without changing your culture overnight.

Humbleness/Modesty/Humaneness

YOU MUST HAVE a healthy ego to lead a company and to lead people. You need high confidence, but it cannot turn into arrogance. When ego turns into arrogance, you lose your ability to read the market, to understand your competitors, or to listen to those around you. You always think you are right and can do no wrong. "Self-contained self confidence" is the key. It is lonely at the top. You must be perceived as a winner, but not tell people how you are a winner. If you have an outgoing personality, you will easily convey "winner", and will need to work on conveying "team". It is tough for some to balance high ego and self confidence and not have it seep into dangerous areas, such as taking the corporate jet on personal trips.

Another big part of leading is being able to put people at ease. It takes some self-deprecating humor to do this. If they are relaxed around you it improves performance and communication. You get the most out of people when they can relax and perform. Humaneness means you care about people. If your direct reports perceive you care about people, they have the potential of deciding to run through brick walls for you. If they believe you do not care about people, they will hesitate to go the extra mile. A level of modesty and humaneness leads to respect as a leader. People emulate you and feel like they learn from you. Patience and dignity carry a CEO through hard times. Never act like you are above everyone else. On the organizational chart, everyone knows you are above everyone else, so if you remind people of it you will come across more as a king than as a leader. You need to see your fellow human as an equal when it does not involve corporate decision making. It is easy for a CEO to view himself/herself above everyone else. You must be perceived as a real person. If you are a nice person, but you don't let people see it, they will perceive the worst. No matter what you really feel, you must go out and show evidence of caring about people, or the rumor will spread like wildfire that you don't care.

Many leaders burn out from faking a level of people compassion/caring that they don't really have. You must know how to make people feel good, you must value their opinion. Don't even think about faking it. Employees will see through it very quickly, and it will cause you plenty of stress along the way. As a leader, you must tolerate the whining and complaining, because a lot of it occurs. And sometimes it happens with your star players. You tell them how great they are, they believe you, and some unfortunately will then cross over to believing they are now more important and worth more than they really are. So the double-edged sword is common here, where you heap praise on your stars and the stars start thinking that they walk on clouds. Now you must deal with their overblown ego, which can result in them drawing a line in the sand and saying "my way or I leave." Since no one person is ever bigger than any company, you now point to the door. They are stunned, in disbelief, and it takes them awhile to reset their ego and figure out what happened. But if you can use your own sense of modesty, you can keep them from going over the edge and prevent it all from happening. So the real value in your own modesty is as a role model, to stop a star from becoming a prima donna. You want empowerment without them actually acting it out. You want them operating as a leader, not actually believing they are the most important person in the organization. You set the culture of "we all put our pants on one leg at a time" and reinforce it with selective empathy for employees. Make them feel as if you care about their career without making them feel as if they are the "chosen one".

You must also set the right tone in the face of bigger events, like a local World Series Championship (take time to celebrate). You find small ways to reward people, whether it is paying for a group lunch, doing something around the holidays, or recognizing birthdays. People need to know you are one of them on the personal side. This is different than trying to be one of them, which never works. Never play the game of "we are all in this boat together" because that is like a private equity CEO who says "my base salary is only $150K, look how many people in the company are above me." Yes, and look how many are above you in shares of stock ownership, none. Don't say things that insult the intelligence of those beneath you. Whenever I hear a start-up CEO say "I have a low base and I want everyone else to have a low base," I want to say, "OK, let's give them all the same amount of equity as well if we are going to be egalitarian about it." The ability to put yourself in their shoes is key to the humble/modesty factor that allows employees to identify with you.

You must be Emotionally Intelligent to act humble. If you have low EI, you cannot suppress your ego and you always need to win. You can't keep stars beneath you if you always need to win, they will leave. One of the most important criteria in a strong leader is the ability to admit when you are wrong. This goes hand-in-hand with the ability to give accolades to others. They carry equal weight. The leader who cannot admit he/she is wrong also has trouble handing out compliments. But never emotionally sink when you admit you are wrong. Everyone is watching to see if your mistake has dented your resiliency. Your confidence level must be strong enough to have minor setbacks roll off your back like water off a duck.

As a recruiter, I always look for a motivation to leave and a motivation to join in a candidate. A very compelling motivation for people to leave a company occurs when they decide that the CEO they are working for is a horse's behind. No counter offer is going to keep them upon resignation, because that CEO is incapable of making them feel valued and wanted by the company. CEOs who are arrogant and mean ultimately lose all their best people and can only keep the ones with the same personality. Unless the stock value is going up real fast, in which case it makes sense to tolerate even Attila the Hun.

Career Management

I GRADUATED FROM BUSINESS school in 1983, and most of our graduating class believed they would eventually be the CEO of a F100 corporation. Twenty-five years later, not one of our classmates made CEO of a F100 corporation. The class ahead of ours landed two in the F100 CEO seat, and those 2 were out inside 3 years after getting the job. It is a tough chair to get and even tougher to keep.

The concept of managing your career is only relevant if you are performing well. If you are good, the organization needs to keep moving you up or you will leave to move up faster elsewhere. If you are happy and satisfied with your current job, and the organization tells you it is time to move up, you could be getting ready for the Peter Principle. As a reminder, the Peter Principle is the old adage that says you will be promoted to the level of your incompetence. This is the ultimate self-test, to turn down a promotion because you know you are not ready. We grow up in a performance-reward society; the goal is to move up as fast as you can. But you fall much further if you fail in a job, way below where you are today before the promotion. If you truly suffer from the Peter Principle, you will get fired from your position. You might have been moved up before you were ready, or you might not have the intellect or skill set to succeed at the next level, no matter how much time you take. You have a 25% chance of hitting the Peter Principle. The ideal promotion means you will have a few years of growth in a job before you become really good at it. The norm is to choose a job and company because you "like it", meaning you like the people, or the products, the services, the industry, something attracted you to the opportunity. You aspire to lead, so you anticipate promotion in your future. Classic examples of the Peter Principle include taking a top salesman and promoting them to sales leader, or promoting a reactive controller to the CFO level, where a proactive business partnership is required with the CEO. You are not supposed to be great at a new job when you first take it, unless you are a serial GM. You are expected to have a quick learning ability, but the job should not become stale inside 2 years.

The goal of any business is to maximize earnings, just like your own personal goal is to maximize personal income. You are in the for-profit business world to make money. If you are not, you should join a not-for-profit. You will likely be presented with at least one major leadership opportunity in life, and you must seize that opportunity if you want to move up as a leader. If you fail to recognize it or pass on it, you will earn far less income than if you seized the chance and capitalized on it. Sometimes it is an internal career move to headquarters, other times it is a chance to take a job on the outside that will dramatically accelerate your career or broaden your scope of responsibilities. Other times it is about accepting a role that will increase your visibility within the organization. Some choose to pass on the next leadership level for lifestyle balance reasons. You must be willing to sacrifice lifestyle if it means a significant jump in leadership responsibilities if your goal is to go as high as you can. If your goal is to climb that corporate ladder, your answer to the promotion that requires a relocation is "yes". Unless you are confident you can get the same leadership opportunity from another company that does not require relocation, your answer is "yes" if you want to climb.

You must also recognize when you have a chance to make a leadership impact. It might be your first presentation to senior management, or your first presentation to the Board. Treat every opportunity to interact with everyone in the company as a chance to show your leadership skills. I interview far too many people who are in a rut and start trudging through the day-to-day. They have become complacent and cynical about their position in corporate life. The problem is that once you get in this mode, your "seize the day' antenna is retracted, and you now have a high probability of missing the internal chance to impress the next level when the opportunity arises. Keep focused on seizing the day at all times. You cannot afford to lose your focus on this long term objective. Mid-career malaise can trap you at your current level. Stay mentally awake and fight off the malaise that John Updike wrote about in his books.

Don't be afraid to proactively test the job market. Get a resume out there into the files of all the search firms. You need to know if the grass is truly greener on the other side. It is your fault if you are stuck, so take some career management responsibility and get proactive about exploring your alternatives. Ideally your job provides the following feelings:

- High self-fulfillment
- Feeling like you make a difference
- Happy day-to-day
- Balanced
- Comfortable within your financial parameters
- Feel like you make a contribution to society
- You make a difference in people's lives
- You have the right lifestyle
- Stress is manageable
- Curveballs are handled
- Constantly achieving short-term goals
- On the path to long-term goals
- High performance/reward environment

Or you could feel the following reality:
- College savings accounts are not fully funded
- Your stock portfolio is down or non-existent
- Your retirement portfolio is down
- Mortgage is too high
- You feel financial stress
- Vacation time is cut back
- You feel pace-of-life stress
- Price of oil, recession, the war with Iraq and Afghanistan, macro stress…
- Your family feels stress – marriage, children, health, aging parents
- Your job feels unfulfilling
- Less time for yourself
- Not enough time to contribute to society
- You feel like the "wagon wheels" are in a rut and they are moving too fast at the same time
- You are not making as much money as you should be

If you feel closer to the second list, it is time to do something about it. Get your resume out to all the retained search firms while you push for an internal promotion. Like a well-known F500 CEO said in his address to the Economic Club of Chicago, "This is America. If you are not successful, it's your own damn fault".

Leadership also comes with significant potential negatives that can stop your forward progress. Avoid the following possible negative aspects of leadership:

- Creating a "churn and burn" environment – doing whatever it takes to get the most out of each subordinate for your own self interest
- Firing a valuable employee because you don't like them
- Demanding crazy hours from subordinates, no life balance allowed
- High ego needs, making people treat you like a king
- The need to win on a daily basis against subordinates
- An authority problem – you can do better than those above
- High degree of distrust of others
- Need for power over others
- The belief that you are above value systems

You can fall into the above leadership traps unless someone is giving you honest feedback. An important aspect of managing your career is identifying someone who is willing to tell you the truth about your leadership skills in each job that you have. Otherwise, you will eventually start believing your own rhetoric. Most people are "muddling through" versus consciously managing their career. If you are good, your career takes care of itself, just like compensation. You need to recognize when an industry/company is not going to be lucrative for you and make a change. You should never stay in a no-win situation. You are only as good as your most recent year of performance.

Summary

I KNOW MULTIPLE CEOs who did not make any real money until their 3rd or 4th company. Sometimes it takes multiple attempts to align your leadership capabilities with the right industry, company, and market timing to hit a "home run". Even if the company is not going to make you wealthy, you can still improve your leadership talents. If you discover over 2–3 years that you cannot improve some critical traits, assess whether you should abandon your general management goals and drop back to leading a function, the function you came from (e.g. marketing, sales, finance, operations, etc). Make sure you give yourself a couple of leadership chances to succeed before backing off. Leadership does not determine success or happiness in life. There are countless successful individual practitioners who do not lead in their day to day professional life: dentists, veterinarians, lawyers, doctors, craftsman, artists, consultants, accountants, recruiters, investment bankers, etc.

But any of these individual practitioners can also choose to become a leader if they lead a team, office, or company. It takes a lot of time, a lot of experience, and a lot of mistakes along the way to become really good at leadership. You can be extremely successful from a financial perspective without managing anyone. There are a lot of "rain maker" careers where the solo superstar makes a lot of money. You must be willing to work hard to become a good leader. It is difficult for really good leaders to accurately explain why they are good. For every Jack Welch, Larry Bossidy, and Rudy Giuliani who go on the book/speaker circuit, there are thousands of leaders of different sized corporations who cannot articulate how they do it, they just do it really well. The key is to figure out early in your career what your leadership weaknesses are, and work hard to improve them. You must also recognize if your weaknesses are too great to accomplish your goals. You will not be happy in your career if you fail every 2 years at leadership, and it won't help that your resume now has warning flags all over it.

You will get paid a lot of money if you are a strong leader. Once you have established your track record of leadership (i.e. you grew sales and profitability above industry norms) your market price will dramatically escalate. We live in a free-market economy, and that means you get paid what you are worth. People who are not in leadership roles are screaming about CEO compensation (which includes exit packages). Those people do not understand that a great CEO candidate has his/her price set by the supply and demand of the market. If the Board and shareholders want the best, they must pay for the best. Think about pro athletes. A superstar can earn millions in his peak career year. If they stay in the game too long and their skills are diminished, the will earn a very small percentage of their peak earnings year. The same is true with leaders. You must maximize your earnings performance at your peak, because your market price will fall as soon as you do not perform well. Publicly traded companies negotiate a large exit package for a strong CEO on the front end because that is what it takes to attract a great CEO. It takes a lot of skill and experience to become a strong CEO, that is why the best get paid more than superstar professional athletes or star entertainers. The public and private markets reward great leadership talent with great compensation packages. This book hopefully creates the self-awareness to allow you to continue improving your leadership skills. As many wealthy leaders exhibit today, the more money you make, the more you can give back to try and improve the world.

Theodore B. Martin, Jr.
Chief Executive Officer

Ted Martin is the Founder and CEO of Martin Partners L.L.C, a leading retained executive search firm. Throughout his twenty plus years as a recruiter, he has been instrumental in building senior management teams, from the Fortune 500 to start-ups. The New Career Makers ranked him as the number one recruiter for venture capital portfolio companies.

He is a Co-Founder and past Chairman of The Alliance Partnership International, a consortium of retained search firms from twenty-three countries across the world. Ted is also a speaker on leadership and executive trends, including: McKinsey & Co.'s CEO Forum, Electronic Commerce World, United Airlines/Hemisphere Magazine, Chicagoland Chamber of Commerce, Kellogg Alumni presentations, Financial Executives Institute and 6Figure Jobs.com Seminar Series. He has presented to numerous senior management teams of private and public corporations.

Ted has been a Board member of the Kellogg Alumni Advisory Board, Chicago Architecture Foundation, Washington & Lee Alumni Board, and Association of Executive Search Consultants (AESC). He is a past Chairman of the USTA Northshore Pro Tennis Tournament, and was a Co-Founder of the Marcy Newberry Auxiliary Board and the St. Gregory's School for Boys Council. Ted is also a member of

The Economic Club, The Chicago Club, The University Club, Illinois Venture Capital Association, Chicagoland Chamber of Commerce. He has received the Kellogg Alumni Service Award and the Washington & Lee Learning, Leadership, and Honor Award. He was Co-Chairman of his 25th class reunion at W&L and Kellogg.

Prior to starting his career in executive search, he held positions in brand management with Wilson Sporting Goods Company and Kraft General Foods. He holds a B.A. from Washington & Lee University and an M.B.A. from Northwestern University's Kellogg Graduate School of Management. Ted and his family reside in a northern suburb of Chicago.

Made in the USA